Thames Essay No. 26

Multinational Enterprises
and the
Third World

BY

V. N. Balasubramanyam

Senior Lecturer in Economics
University of Lancaster

TRADE POLICY RESEARCH CENTRE
1 Gough Square
London EC4A 3DE

The photograph on the front cover shows Astral skin cream being manufactured and packaged at the factory in Apapa, Lagos, of Lever Brothers
Nigeria, an associated company of Unilever which has companies in over
seventy countries all around the world.

ISSN 0306-6991
ISBN 0 900842 48 2

Printed in the United Kingdom by
Ditchling Press Limited
Hassocks, Sussex

First published 1980

Contents

List of Tables

Biographical Note

V. N. BALASUBRAMANYAM, a specialist on policy problems in the field of international direct investment, is a Senior Lecturer in Economics at the University of Lancaster which he joined in 1969. Before going to the United States for graduate studies in 1964, he was an economist with the Indian Statistical Institute in New Delhi, attached to the Indian Planning Commission.

His principal works include *International Transfer of Technology to India* (1973) and, with Alasdair I. MacBean, *Meeting the Third World Challenge* (1976 and 1978), published for the Trade Policy Research Centre, as well as a study entitled *A Positive Approach to the New International Economic Order: Non-trade Issues* (1980), also with Professor MacBean.

Preface

THE ROLE of multinational enterprises in the development of the world economy continues to feature in discussions on the international economic order, in spite of
the enormous literature that has developed on the subject,
putting in perspective most if not all of the issues, both
real and imagined, which have been raised over the last
two or three decades in connection with firms operating
in one or more foreign countries. When in the mid-1970s
the developing countries advanced proposals for a 'new
international economic order' (NIEO) in the United
Nations and its agencies, attention focussed mainly on commodity price-stabilisation schemes and other commodity-
related issues, but the NIEO programme has also included
proposals on the operations of multinational enterprises
and on the transfer of technology that is entailed. The
NIEO proposals were given a new lease of life with the
publication of the Report of the Independent Commission
on International Development Issues, entitled *North-
South: a Programme for Survival*, but usually referred to as
the Brandt Report, the Chairman of the Commission
having been Willy Brandt, the former Chancellor of the
Federal Republic of Germany.

V. N. Balasubramanyam, co-author of *Meeting the
Third World Challenge*, first published for the Trade Policy
Research Centre in 1976 (the second edition appearing
in 1978), deals in this Thames Essay with the central

issues in the North-South debate that relate to multi-national enterprises, private direct investment and the transfer of technology, to which the Brandt Report devotes a chapter without breaking any new ground.

The Brandt Report discusses (i) the importance of multinational enterprises in world production, the processing of raw materials and trade, (ii) the consequent significance of private direct investment in capital flows to developing countries and (iii) the opportunities, by which is meant requirements, for improved cooperation between multinational enterprises and the governments of 'home' and 'host' countries in increasing flows of investment and transfers of technology. The report views these relationships as prone to mutual suspicion and mistrust which is thus liable to produce conflicts and inhibit investment. As a result, the Brandt Report sees a mutuality of interest in the establishment, if possible by contractual means, of a regime for international investment.

Clear guidelines for international investment, together with greater access to information about the relative merits of different technologies and different managements, might be expected to strengthen the bargaining position of the governments of developing countries in negotiations with multinational enterprises. Criteria which would sharpen the ability of governments to evaluate competitive bids cannot be opposed in the context of an international economic order based on market principles. Inter-governmental organisations could play a role in this respect and, indeed, the World Bank is already stressing, in its lending for minerals and energy development, the need for governments to be better informed.

In its report, the Brandt Commission argues that more effective regulation of transfer-pricing and restrictive business practices, among other aspects of the operations of multinational enterprises, are necessary in order to minimise the costs of direct investment and to ensure that the benefits of the transfer of capital and technology accrue to developing countries in increased production, employment and trade. This position only differs from that of the Organisation for Economic Cooperation and Development (OECD), where the developed countries are represented, in that greater faith is attached to mandatory regulations than to a voluntary code of conduct. Nothing is presented, however, to support the belief that mandatory regulations would result in a more effective transfer of technology and a more efficient allocation and use of resources. Nor is anything said on the question which is more fundamental to private investment, whether generated internally or attracted from abroad, namely the economic and political stability of the country seeking economic development.

If multinational enterprises are seen as agencies of economic development, their growth in numbers and size reflecting the rapid integration of the world economy over the last three decades, then they can also be seen to represent a 'package' of capital, technical 'know-how' and managerial expertise. 'Unbundling' the package can be achieved to a certain extent and, as the Brandt Report notes, has been taking place. Increased activity of this kind reflects 'efforts towards greater technological self-reliance' and perhaps, as the Brandt Report suggests, such self-reliance in appropriate technologies should be supported through international cooperation. Indeed, the Brandt Report conveys the impression that inter-governmental agencies should provide an alternative to multinational enterprises as a source of technology, but too great a reliance on sources other than direct investments of multinational enterprises could prove to be very costly. Activities of inter-governmental organisations and those of multinational enterprises should perhaps be seen as complementary.

Be that as it may, Dr Balasubramanyam's Thames Essay seeks to clarify the issues raised in the NIEO programme and, later, in the Brandt Report. It was prepared as part of a programme of studies on the NIEO proposals that was conducted by the Trade Policy Research Centre with the help of a major grant from the Ford Foundation in New York. The Centre has greatly appreciated this support from the Ford Foundation which has done much to encourage research on international economic issues.

It has to be stressed, as usual, that the views expressed in this Thames Essay do not necessarily reflect the views of members of the Council or those of staff and associates of the Trade Policy Research Centre which, having general terms of reference, does not represent on any particular issue a consensus of opinion. The purpose of the Centre is to promote independent research and public discussion of international economic affairs.

HUGH CORBET
Director
Trade Policy Research Centre

London
March 1980

CHAPTER ONE

Foreign Private Investment in Development Theories

MULTINATIONAL enterprises and their role in the transfer of technology from developed to developing countries has figured prominently in 'the North-South debate' as it has evolved since the mid-1970s. It is a subject which has been hotly argued between governments and is usually high on the agenda of United Nations conferences on economic affairs.[1]

This essay analyses the main issues concerning the multinational enterprise and the transfer of technology as it has been raised in the North-South debate, most notably in the Declaration on the Establishment of a New International Economic Order (NIEO), a resolution of the United Nations in 1974 that advanced a programme of specific proposals,[2] some of which have dropped by the wayside,[3] but others of which have come to form part of the basis for a continuing debate on the reform of the international system of trade and payments, which has been given a boost by the report of the Independent Commission on International Development Issues (the Brandt Report).[4] The object of the essay is to clarify the issues and arrive at some policy proposals which might weather the storms of North-South exchanges.

Theories and models are not only rife in the sphere of development economics. They also appear to be subject to a high degree of obsolescence. In the early phase of development economics, savings and capital accumulation were accorded a strategic role in the development process. The models in vogue were those which linked rates of growth to savings and investment. These were soon to be superseded by 'structural imbalance' theories. Popular in the 1960s were models emphasising foreign-exchange shortages as a bottleneck in the development process. The current preoccupation is with technology. Models linking rates of growth to savings and foreign exchange have yielded to technology-transfer models. Increasingly, the emphasis is on the contribution of the intangible factors of production—technology, human skills and entrepreneurship—to the development process, as opposed to the early concern of development economics with financial factors.

It is significant that foreign private investment has survived as a part of this changing panorama in one guise or another. When models centred on savings and foreign-exchange considerations held the stage, foreign private investment was looked upon as a source of savings and foreign exchange; it could bridge the savings gap and the foreign-exchange gap. Now that technical change is regarded as the engine of development, foreign private investment is regarded as a major conduit for transferring technology and 'know-how' from the developed to the developing countries.

Positive Role of Multinational
Enterprises

Indeed, the potential of foreign private investment as a mechanism for the transfer of technology has been acknowledged by differing ideological approaches to the development problem. It is not surprising that those who subscribe to the view that development can be speeded up by integrating the developing countries into the international economic system should assign a key role to foreign private investment and its manifestation through the operations of multinational enterprises. A multinational enterprise is defined as an enterprise which owns or controls producing facilities in more than one country.[5]

But even those who are disenchanted with the contribution to the development process of the international order, as it was established after World War II, perceive a positive role—if only a transient one—for the multinational enterprise. According to this view, underdevelopment is caused, and also perpetuated, by the dependence of the developing countries on the developed countries. This dependence, it is said, is fundamentally technological in nature. The elimination of dependence requires the international diffusion of technology; and the instrument of such diffusion is the multinational enterprise. As a recent study subscribing to the 'dependence' view of development puts it: 'The multinational is perhaps the only organisation that will in the near future be capable of generating massive flows of embodied and disembodied "hardware" and "software" technology to the developing countries. In a world where aid and technical assistance programmes are shrinking daily, the multinational will in all likelihood increase in importance as the agent of technology transfer to the developing countries.'[6]

The technology and managerial expertise which accompanies foreign private investment has long been acknowledged to be its distinguishing characteristic. The advent of the multinational enterprise, often acclaimed as the most significant twentieth-century institutional innovation, has endowed foreign private investment with a high degree of flexibility and adaptability. The significance of the geographical spread and flexibility of multinational enterprises is made clear by the more elaborate definition provided by a leading American scholar on the subject, Raymond Vernon, of Harvard

3

University: 'It is a parent company that controls a large cluster of corporations of various nationalities. The corporations that make up each cluster appear to have access to a common pool of human and financial resources and seem responsive to elements of a common strategy. Size is important as well; a cluster of this sort with less than $100 million in sales rarely merits much attention.'[7]

It is these characteristics that have endowed multinational enterprises with the ability to generate massive flows of technology to the developing countries. Their size and command over resources in different parts of the world enables them to reap economies of scale in the production and distribution of knowledge. Their geographical dispersion and ability to respond to a common strategy allows them to share the costs and benefits of their activities between the countries in which they operate. These characteristics allow them to reap the advantage of geographical specialisation and integration.

The very strengths of multinational enterprises, however, have also proved to be their curse. Their size and the control they exercise over operations are seen to pose a threat to the political sovereignty and economic independence of the new nation-states of the Third World. Their search for profitable opportunities, and their emphasis on cost minimisation and efficiency, are seen to be inimical to considerations of social justice and equity, however they are defined. Concern is expressed that their activities may thwart rather than promote national economic objectives such as the reduction of income disparities, increased employment opportunities and strengthened balance of payments. More significantly, the *modus operandi* of their operations, which is confined to the internal bureaucracy of the enterprise transcending the market, is seen to pose serious problems in the area of pricing of technologies and products and in the distribution of gains between the corporations and the host countries.

4

Paradoxical as it may seem, then, multinational enterprises are at one and the same time hailed as agents of change and condemned as instruments of exploitation. It is, however, significant that both the developing countries and multinational enterprises are recognising the need for coexistence and are, it might be hoped, entering an era of negotiation and understanding instead of one of distrust and confrontation. The challenge facing policy makers is how best to harness the acknowledged prowess of the multinational enterprise as an agent of change without, in the process, undermining its very abilities to do so.

This was the central issue posed by the approach to foreign private investment and technology transfer in the United Nations declaration on the 'new international economic order'. The declaration repeatedly affirmed the need for access to modern technology on the part of the developing countries. Implicit in the declaration was also faith in the ability of foreign private enterprise to provide such technology. The thrust of the declaration, however, was on the need to regulate and reform the operations and organisational features of foreign private investment.

The issues posed in the declaration covered a wide spectrum ranging from the pricing of imported technologies to the need for an international code of conduct on technology transfers. The demands made in the declaration reflected many of the long simmering grievances of the developing countries towards foreign private investment and technology transfers. Many of these grievances were and remain real. But many arose out of emotive considerations and an insufficient understanding of the economic forces underlying foreign private investment and technology transmission. While multinational enterprises were and are answerable for a lot, there is also the real danger that hasty and ill-conceived regulations

5

and restrictions may undermine their acknowledged ability to effect the international transfer of technology. Hence there is a need for a close examination of the main issues that pertain to foreign private investment and international transfer of technology in the NIEO proposals—issues that are still vital to the continuing debate on the reform of the international economic order.

Chapter 2 discusses some of the recent theoretical explanations of foreign private investment and multinational enterprises which have a bearing on many of the issues relating to the transfer of technology. It also provides a brief sketch of the nature and magnitude of foreign private investment in the developing countries. Chapter 3 summarises the nature of the international market in technology and discusses the problems surrounding the pricing of imported technologies. Chapter 4 discusses the issue of 'inappropriateness' of imported technologies. Chapter 5 analyses the viability of alternative market-oriented mechanisms, to the multinational enterprise, for the transmission of technology or what has come to be known as the issue of 'unbundling the foreign investment package'. Chapter 6 discusses the main conclusions of the analysis with a view to formulating policy proposals.

NOTES AND REFERENCES

1.Indeed, the transfer of technology was a central issue in a whole United Nations conference devoted to science and technology, held in Vienna, in August 1979. The conference was not hailed by anybody as a great success.

2.See the *Declaration on the Establishment of a New International Economic Order*, and the programme of action set out in a separate document, drawn up at the sixth special session of the General Assembly of the United Nations, New York, April-May 1974, the original thrust of which was 'an integrated commodity programme' designed to bring about a transfer of resources from rich to poor countries through engineering higher commodity prices in an attempt to follow the example of the Organisation of Petroleum Exporting Countries (OPEC).

For an early critique of this approach to the promotion of the development of the world economy, see Hugh Corbet, *Raw Materials: Beyond the*

Rhetoric of Commodity Power, International Issues No. 1 (London: Trade Policy Research Centre, 1975).

3.The NIEO proposals generated a considerable literature, but even if some of the political expressions associated with the proposals have lost much of their force, the basic economic issues remain. For a clear and succinct assessment of the proposals, see W. M. Corden, *The NIEO Proposals: a Cool Look*, Thames Essay No. 19 (London: Trade Policy Research Centre, 1979). For a fuller assessment of the basic economic issues of development, see Alasdair I. MacBean and V. N. Balasubramanyam, *Meeting the Third World Challenge* (London: Macmillan, for the Trade Policy Research Centre, 1978).

4.Independent Commission on International Development Issues, *North-South: a Programme for Survival*, Brandt Report (London: Pan Books, 1980). The Chairman of the Commission was Mr Willy Brandt, the former Chancellor of the Federal Republic of Germany.

5.John H. Dunning (ed.), *The Multinational Enterprise* (London: Allen & Unwin, 1971) p. 16. It might be added that, strictly speaking, there is no such thing as a multinational corporation, only national corporations or companies which are affiliated with one another in groups, namely multi-national enterprises.

6.Hans Singer and Javed Ansari, *Rich and Poor Countries* (London: Allen & Unwin, 1977), p. 209.

7.Raymond Vernon, *Sovereignty at Bay* (New York: Basic Books, 1971) p. 4.

CHAPTER TWO

Theoretical Explanations of Private Foreign Investment

WHY DO firms go abroad? What are the factors motivating foreign private investment and the spread of multinational enterprises? These questions have been the focus of a growing body of literature spanning the branches of industrial organisation theory, international trade theory and the theory of the firm. The insights into the nature and methods of operations of the multinational enterprise provided by these theoretical explanations have a bearing on the currently debated issues relating to foreign private investment and transfers of technology. A brief discussion of these theoretical explanations for foreign private investment will help place these issues in perspective.

One of the most widely-known explanations for foreign private investment, advanced by the late Stephen Hymer and Charles P. Kindleberger, of the Massachusetts Institute of Technology, is the monopoly over advantages that the foreign firms possess.[1] These advantages range from access to patented and generally unavailable technology, team-specific managerial skills, plant economies of scale and special marketing skills to the possession of a brand name. It is the desire to exploit these advantages in foreign markets that explains the decision to set up production facilities abroad. Foreign investment would be preferred to licensing the advantages or exporting the product, as it enables the firm to capture fully the rent accruing from its monopoly over advantages. Licensing the advantages would be an inferior alternative to foreign private investment because of the imperfections in the markets for patents and other forms of knowledge. Production abroad is preferred to production at home and export as it enables the firm to exploit differences in factor prices and overcome tariff barriers and transport costs. Nearness to markets also enables the firm to adapt and modify the product to suit local conditions and tastes. In fact a variant of the industrial organisation approach explains foreign private investment in terms of the ability of oligopolistic firms to differentiate either the same product across different regions or differentiate a wide range of products in one region, or even a mix of the two.[2]

PRODUCT-CYCLE THEORY

The most widely discussed trade-theory approach to the explanation of foreign private investment is the product-cycle hypothesis advanced by Professor Vernon.[3] According to this thesis, the life of a product can be broken into three stages: (i) the innovative new product stage, (ii) the maturing product stage and (iii) the standardised product stage. In the first stage both demand and supply conditions require the locus of production to be in the developed countries. On the demand side, high levels of income and rising labour costs in these countries generate a demand for differentiated products and labour-saving goods. On the supply side, the skill and research intensity of new products endow the developed countries with a comparative advantage in their production. Moreover, at this stage of the product, there is a need for frequent communication between production and marketing. In the second stage of the product, the technology becomes stabilised, economies of scale emerge and the products become price elastic. As new markets emerge they are first serviced by exports. Cost considerations become important at this stage and, depending on labour-cost differentials, production facilities are moved

9

to other high-income countries with demand patterns similar to those at home. In the final stage, the product is totally undifferentiated. Little interaction is needed between the producers and consumers and competition is based solely on price. Cost considerations are of great significance and, therefore, production facilities are moved to developing countries to take advantage of low labour costs. At this stage, third markets, and even the home market, may be serviced from the developing countries.

The more recent firm-theory approach to an explanation of the multinational enterprise draws together several of the strands of the earlier theories. This approach, first enunciated by Peter Buckley and Mark Casson, of the University of Reading, explains the multinational enterprise as a response to the imperfect nature of the markets in intermediate inputs, including the market for knowledge.[4] Such markets are imperfect in the sense that they are difficult to organise, pose serious problems of uncertainty and they often preclude pricing arrangements by which rent-yielding advantages can be fully exploited. In order to by-pass these imperfections in the external markets, enterprises internalise their operations; in other words, enterprises resort to backward and forward integration to overcome market imperfections.

MARKET FOR KNOWLEDGE

The incentives to internalise are especially strong in the market for various types of knowledge. The creation of new processes and products involves lengthy time lags, is subject to a high degree of uncertainty and involves considerable investment. The nature of the activity is such that it requires detailed long-term planning and coordination. Information on avoiding mistakes is more difficult and costly to transmit through the market than on an intra-enterprise basis. Moreover, knowledge exhibits the characteristics of a public good: once it is produced it becomes a 'free good'; the use of it does not diminish the stock and it cannot be appropriated by individuals. The market for knowledge is imperfect in the sense that it does not enable the producer of knowledge to fully appropriate the rent from the production of knowledge. The incentive to internalise, arising from the imperfect nature of the market for knowledge, is succinctly stated by Stephen P. Magee, of the University of Texas at Austin: 'Multinational corporations are large because it is more efficient to transfer information on development from product to product within the firm rather than through the market. Also the public goods nature of such information dictates that firms expand to internalise the externality of such information.'[5]

The accent of the theoretical explanations of the multinational enterprise, briefly sketched, is on technology. While these go a long way in explaining the technology-generating abilities of foreign firms and the *modus operandi* of multinational enterprises, they also suggest the problems their operations give rise to, especially in the context of the development problem.

PRICING OF PRODUCTS

The first of these problems relates to the pricing of products and technologies produced by the multinational enterprises. What component of the prices charged constitutes a reward for their investment in research and development, the rents from which, theoretically, the enterprises cannot fully recoup in external markets; and what component of the prices are pure monopoly gains unrelated to the costs they incur in generating new products and processes? There is also the much-discussed issue of transfer-pricing. When transactions covering sales of technology and various intermediate inputs take place between units of the same

11

enterprise rather than through external markets, it provides the firm with an opportunity to price them above the price that can be obtained in external markets. Such a strategy enables the firm to manipulate and shift profits from one area of operation to another with a view to minimising its tax burden. It is recognised that one of the advantages to internalisation lies in the opportunities it provides the enterprise to avoid government intervention and regulation.[6]

Apart from the problem of pricing there is the question of the 'appropriateness' of the products and technologies produced by multinational enterprises to the needs and conditions prevailing in the developing countries. While the ability of multinationals to transfer technology is acknowledged, doubts are often expressed about the quality of the technology they transmit. The theoretical explanations, save that of Professor Vernon, have little to say on this issue; and Professor Vernon's analysis appears to cut both ways. According to the product-cycle hypothesis, it is in the final standardised stage in the life of the product that production facilities are moved to the developing countries. At this stage it is labour costs that are significant. Scientific and technical inputs are relatively unimportant and the comparative advantage of developing countries based on cheap unskilled and semi-skilled labour comes into play. Technologies which are operated in conjunction with such unskilled and semi-skilled labour could hardly be held to be inappropriate to the developing countries. Equally, it can be argued that by the time the product has reached the standardised stage, production functions would have frozen and there would be little room for the substitution of unskilled labour for other inputs.

Beyond these specific issues, relating to pricing and inappropriateness of the technologies transmitted by multinational enterprises, the theoretical explanations also raise more general issues. Market imperfections are the seed bed of multinationals according to these theories. In the Hymer-Kindleberger approach, establishing production facilities abroad is preferable to other methods of exploiting the monopoly over rent-yielding advantages that the enterprise possesses because of imperfections in the market for knowledge. The more elaborate Buckley-Casson analysis is also in the same vein. But, it can be argued, if production abroad and internalisation of operations serve the interests of multinational enterprises, do they also serve the interests of developing countries? And would developing countries be better off buying the various components of the foreign private investment package in external markets—imperfect as they may be? They could, it has been suggested, borrow the capital on international markets and purchase the technology from foreign firms through licensing agreements and management contracts. Beyond this is the wider and somewhat hypothetical question: would resource allocation have been more efficient than it is in the absence of the multinational enterprise? In other words, in their attempts to over come and exploit market imperfections, have multinational enterprises introduced a new set of imperfections?

The theoretical explanations are, for the most part, neutral on these issues. Their concern is with elucidating the characteristics of multinational enterprises, the source of their strength and their methods of operation. They can be said to belong to the realm of positive economics. Their emphasis is more on considerations of efficiency rather than equity. They provide, however, a framework for analysing what are essentially normative issues such as the distribution of gains from foreign private investment between the multinationals and the host countries. Value judgments are unavoidable in analysing these issues. But in the absence of an understanding of the nature and characteristics of foreign private investment, value judgments may override objectivity. Before analysing, in

13

detail, the specific issues raised above it would be in order to examine the magnitude and sectoral distribution of foreign private investment in the developing countries.

DISTRIBUTION OF FOREIGN PRIVATE
INVESTMENT

In spite of the burgeoning literature on foreign private investment, statistics on its size and scope are sadly inadequate, particularly in the case of investment in developing countries. The most comprehensive data on the share of different countries in the total stock of foreign private investment is that published by the United Nations for the year 1967 and some of this data has been updated by the United Nations Commission on Transnational Corporations in 1978.

The total book value of foreign private investment held by the market-oriented economies at the end of 1975 came to $259,000 million, with the United States accounting for 48 per cent, followed by the United Kingdom with 12 per cent, then by Japan, Switzerland and West Germany with around 6 per cent each and France and Canada with around 4 per cent each of the total (Table 2.1).

The developing countries, as a whole, accounted for $68,000 million of the estimated stock of foreign private investment (26 per cent of the total) at the end of 1975, the latest year for which the United Nations provides figures. The latest estimates published by the Organisation for Economic Cooperation and Development (OECD) show that the total stock of foreign private investment in developing countries had increased to $76,000 million at the end of 1976. It is also reported that between 1970 and 1976 the annual average rate of growth of such investment was around 13 per cent. Detailed data on the share of major investors in the total stock at the end of the year 1976 are not available.

TABLE 2.1   Market Economies: Stock of Foreign Private Investment
(book value, 1967, 1971 and 1975)

Country	1967 $m	1967 per cent	1971 $m	1971 per cent	1975 $m	1975 per cent
United States	59,486	55.0	86,001	52.0	124,200	47.8
United Kingdom	17,521	16.2	24,019	14.5	30,800	11.9
France	6,000	5.5	9,540	5.8	11,100	4.3
West Germany	3,015	2.8	7,276	4.4	16,000	6.2
Switzerland	4,250	3.9	6,760	4.1	16,900	6.5
Canada	3,728	3.4	5,930	3.6	10,500	4.1
Japan	1,458	1.3	4,480	2.7	15,900	6.1
Netherlands	2,250	2.1	3,580	2.2	8,300	3.2
Sweden	1,514	1.4	3,450	2.1	4,400	1.7
Italy	2,110	1.9	3,350	2.0	3,300	1.3
Belgium	2,040	0.4	3,250	2.0		
Australia	380	1.9	610	0.4		
Portugal	200	0.2	320	0.2	na	
Denmark	190	0.2	310	0.2		
Norway	60	0.0	90	0.0		
Austria	30	0.0	40	0.0		
Other	4,000	3.7	6,000	3.6	15,100	5.7
TOTAL	108,200	100.0	65,000	100.0	258,900	100.00

SOURCE: *Multinational Corporations in World Development* (New York: United Nations, 1973) p. 139; and *Transnational Corporations in World Development* (New York: United Nations Commission on Transnational Corporations, 1978) p. 236.

In 1967, the year for which comprehensive data for source country and recipients are available, the developing countries as a whole accounted for $33,000 million out of the total stock of foreign private investment estimated at $165,000 million. The United States was the leading investor in the developing countries with a 50 per cent share, the bulk of it concentrated in Latin America, followed by the United Kingdom with a 20 per cent share, with much of its investment being in Africa and Asia. Table 2.2 shows the distribution of foreign private investment in developing countries by country of origin and recipient region.

TABLE 2.2

Foreign Private Investment Stock in Developing
Countries by Country of Origin and Developing
Region, 1967
(per cent)

Country of origin	Recipient region				
	Middle East	Asia	Africa	Latin America	Total
Total: ($m)	3,102.7	4,991.5	6,591.1	18,449.3	33,134.6
Share of major investors (per cent)	(9.4)	(15.0)	(20.0)	(55.6)	(100.0)
United States	57.3	35.6	20.8	63.8	50.4
United Kingdom	27.1	41.5	30.0	9.2	19.9
France	5.2	6.6	26.3	2.5	8.1
Netherlands	5.6	5.1	4.9	5.1	5.1
Canada	0.2	1.0	0.7	7.3	3.1
Japan	2.7	3.9	0.2	2.2	2.1
Italy	0.8	0.6	3.8	2.1	2.7
Belgium	0.1	0.3	7.3	0.6	1.9
Switzerland	0.2	1.4	0.9	2.3	1.7
Others	0.1	2.6	3.0	0.6	1.3

SOURCE: *Multinational Corporations in World Development* (New York: United Nations, 1973).

16

The concentration of the United States' investment in Latin America, Britain's in Asia and Africa, France's in Africa and Japan's in Asia is largely explained by past political and economic ties. These aggregate figures for the major regions, however, mask a significant feature of foreign private investment: its concentration in a few countries in each of the regions. In Latin America, Brazil (20.2 per cent), Venezuela (18.9 per cent), Argentina (9.9 per cent) and Mexico (9.7 per cent) together accounted for nearly 59 per cent of the total stock of foreign private investment in the region. In Asia, India (26.2 per cent), the Philippines (14.5 per cent), Malaysia (13.6 per cent), Pakistan (6.9 per cent) and Hong Kong (5.7 per cent) accounted for 67 per cent of the total investment in the region. In Africa, five countries, Nigeria (16.8 per cent), Algeria (10.7 per cent), Libya (8.8 per cent), Zaire (7.3 per cent) and Zambia (6.4 per cent) accounted for 50 per cent of the total stock of foreign investment in the region. The latest available estimates for 1976 show that the pattern has not altered much although Brazil and Mexico in the Latin American region and Indonesia, Hong Kong, Singapore and South Korea in the Asian region have experienced an appreciable increase in their stock of foreign private capital (see Table 2.3).

This geographic concentration of foreign private investment is the result of a complex set of economic and political factors. It is explained by the sectoral composition of foreign private investment, the economic policies of the host countries and the 'climate' they provide for such investment. A characteristic feature of foreign private investment is its concentration in the petroleum and the manufacturing sectors. At the end of 1967, 33 per cent of the total stock of foreign private investment in the developing countries was in petroleum, 29 per cent in manufacturing, 11 per cent in mining and 5.2 per cent in

TABLE 2.3

Distribution of Stock of Foreign Private Investment
(per cent)

	1967	1976
Latin America		
Brazil	20.2	27.3
Venezuela	18.9	8.7
Argentina	9.9	6.8
Mexico	9.7	14.0
Asia		
India	26.2	13.0
Philippines	14.5	7.3
Malaysia	13.6	12.5
Pakistan	6.9	4.0
Hong Kong	5.7	7.7
Indonesia	5.1	26.6
Thailand	4.3	1.8
Singapore	3.7	6.9
South Korea	1.6	6.0
Africa		
Nigeria	16.8	10.4
Algeria	10.7	4.1
Libya	8.8	5.1
Zaire	7.3	11.5
Zambia	6.4	3.1
Kenya	2.6	5.2

SOURCE: *Multinational Corporations in World Development* (New York: United Nations, 1973) for 1967 figures and *OECD Development Corporation, 1978 Review* (Paris: OECD Secretariat, 1978) for 1976 figures.

agriculture. Public utilities and the services sector accounted for the rest. The OECD estimates for the year 1970 show a similar pattern of sectoral distribution. Table 2.4 shows the sectoral distribution of the stock of foreign private investment at the end of 1967 classified by the major developing regions.

Investments in petroleum and mining account for the predominant shares of Nigeria, Algeria, Libya, Zaire and

TABLE 2.4

Sectoral Distribution of Stock of Foreign Private Investment in the Developing Regions, 1967

	Africa		Western hemisphere		Asia		Middle East	
	$m	per cent	$m	per cent	$m	per cent	$m	per cent
Petroleum	2,597.6	39.4	4,485.5	24.3	1,102.3	22.1	2,776.4	89.5
Manufacturing	1,236.4	18.8	6,652.7	36.1	1,547.7	31.0	190.3	6.1
Mining	1,279.8	19.4	2,016.1	10.9	252.5	5.1	6.0	0.2
Trade	398.2	6.0	1,668.3	9.0	504.4	10.1	30.0	1.0
Agriculture	496.8	7.5	607.4	3.3	939.1	18.8	2.5	0.1
Public utilities	66.3	1.0	1,370.7	7.4	123.0	2.4	10.5	0.3
Others	516.1	8.9	1,648.6	9.0	522.5	10.5	87.0	2.8
Total	6,591.1	100.0	18,449.3	100.0	4,991.5	100.0	3,102.7	100.0

SOURCE: *Multinational Corporations in World Development* (New York: United Nations, 1973) p. 177.

19

Zambia in the African region. In all these countries the stock of investment in either petroleum or mining is reported to exceed $200 million. In Latin America and Asia, manufacturing is the predominant sector of investment. In Brazil, Argentina, Mexico, India and the Philippines, the stock of foreign investment in manufacturing is reported to exceed $200 million.

Petroleum and mineral resources of the African countries listed above largely account for the concentration of foreign investment in these countries. Much of the foreign private investment in the Asian and Latin American countries listed above, with the exception of Venezuela, is mainly in the manufacturing sector. It is the size of their markets, their record of industrialisation and their attitudes towards foreign private investment that explains their significant share. Brazil, Argentina, Mexico and India along with Spain are the so-called 'Big Five' developing countries. Together they are reported to have accounted for 60 per cent of all foreign manufacturing investment in the developing countries at the end of 1967. All these countries have had a long history of industrialisation and the focus of their industrialisation in recent years has increasingly been on the technologically-intensive sectors such as steel, chemicals, pharmaceuticals, transport equipment and capital goods. These are the industries in which foreign manufacturing investment, especially that of the United States, predominates.

The import-substituting industrialisation policies of most of these countries have also provided the foreign firms with profitable markets sheltered from international competition by tariffs and quotas. Although their attitudes towards foreign investment have vacillated, and they have imposed restrictions of various sorts on the operations of foreign firms, they have not been entirely hostile. In fact, the attitude of Pakistan, the Philippines and Malaysia, the major recipients of foreign investment apart from India in the Asian region, can be described as hospitable.

INVESTMENT IN THE MANUFACTURING SECTOR

A recent feature of foreign private investment in the manufacturing sector, whose ramifications have been the focus of extensive debate and discussion, is export-oriented investment.[7] Although such investment is of significant proportions, mainly in Hong Kong, Taiwan, South Korea and Singapore, it is gathering strength in Mexico, Brazil and India. Export-oriented investments are largely for the manufacture of components of manufactured goods to be assembled elsewhere. Apart from the availability of relatively cheap, but high quality, labour in these countries, their low tariff rates on imports and the climate they provide for foreign private investment have played a significant role in attracting such investment. Recent trends show a surge of foreign private investment in these countries (see Table 2.5).

TABLE 2.5

Stock of Foreign Private Investment in Selected
Asian Countries
($ million)

	1967	1976
South Korea	78	1150
Taiwan	—	1670
Singapore	183	1330
Hong Kong	285	1480
Malaysia	679	2400
Philippines	723	1400

SOURCE: *Multinational Corporations in World Development* (New York: United Nations, 1973) for 1967 figures; and *OECD Development Corporation, 1978 Review* (Paris: OECD Secretariat, 1978) for 1976 figures.

The sectoral composition of foreign private investment in the developing countries in general appears to be changing increasingly in favour of the manufacturing sector. Table 2.6 shows the composition of United States foreign private investment in the developing countries as a whole for the years 1967 and 1975. The total book value of foreign investment of the United States at the end of 1975 was around $133,000 million of which 68 per cent was in the developed countries and 32 per cent in the developing countries.

TABLE 2.6

Sectoral Distribution of United States Foreign Private Investment in the Developing Countries, 1967 and 1975 (per cent)

Sector	1967	1975
Petroleum	36.4	32.0
Manufacturing	24.5	30.0
Mining	12.2	6.2
Services	15.3	25.0
Others	10.7	6.8

SOURCES: Figures for 1967 were estimated from data in *Multinationals in World Development* (New York: United Nations, 1973); and for 1975 from data in 'US Direct Investment Abroad in 1975', *Survey of Current Business*, Washington, August 1976, Vol. 56, No. 8.

Available data for the pattern of foreign private investments of the United Kingdom for the year 1971 show that 41 per cent of all such investment in the developing countries was in the manufacturing sector and that the total value of British foreign private investment was £6,667 million, with 72 per cent going to the developed countries and 28 per cent to the developing countries. The composition of foreign private investment within the manufacturing sector indicates its concentration in the skill-intensive industries in which research and development is important. This is especially so in the case of American investment and, to a lesser extent, in the case of British investment. Table 2.7 shows the classification of the two countries' foreign manufacturing investment by major industry groups.

TABLE 2.7

Composition of United States and United Kingdom Foreign Private Investment in the Manufacturing Sector (per cent)

Sector	United States (1975)		United Kingdom (1971)	
	Developed countries	Developing countries	Developed countries	Developing countries
Food product	8.4	8.8	26.5	34.4
Chemicals	18.4	25.5	18.0	14.8
Metal manufactures	6.1	8.3	4.0	2.2
Machinery	29.3	22.2	21.0	10.5
Transport equipment	15.3	11.4	2.2[a]	3.0[a]
Other manufacturing	22.0	23.8	29.3	31.4

SOURCES: 'US Direct Investment Abroad in 1975', *Survey of Current Business*, Washington, August 1976, Vol. 56, No. 8; and *Business Monitor: Overseas Transactions* (London: HM Stationery Office, 1974).

[a]The category 'transport equipment' for United Kingdom relates to motor vehicles only.

There is some difference between the American and British pattern of investment in the manufacturing sector. The former is much more heavily concentrated in the technologically-intensive sectors such as chemicals, machinery and transport equipment; the latter is directed more towards the relatively less technological-intensive industries like food products and textiles (grouped under 'other manufacturing'). The West German and Swiss investments are also directed at the technologically-intensive industries, while Japanese investment is directed at relatively less technologically-intensive industries such as textiles, lumber and pulp and non-ferrous metals.

Concentration of Investment

A dominant theme in the literature on foreign private investment is its concentration in a limited number of multi-national enterprises. Table 2.8 shows that over 150 enterprises account for more than 50 per cent of all

TABLE 2.8

Parent Enterprise Concentration of Foreign Direct Investment

			Concentration		
Home country	*1971 stock of foreign direct investment ($m)*	*Number of transnational enterprises*	*Year*	*Per cent of foreign direct investment accounted for*	*Amount of 1971 stock of foreign investment accounted for by specified number of enterprises ($m)*
United States	86,000	50	1966	55	47,300
United Kingdom	24,000	52	1962	71	17,100
West Germany	7,300	24	1964	52	3,900
Switzerland	6,800	7	1965	65	4,400
Canada	5,900	13	1963	70	4,200
Japan	4,500	20	1972	28	1,300
Sweden	3,500	5	1965	50	1,700
Total	138,000	171		58	79,900
World total	165,000	over 10,000	1969-1970	100	165,000

SOURCE: Karl P. Sauvant, 'The Potential of Multinational Enterprises as Vehicles for the Transmission of Business Culture', in Karl P. Sauvant and Farid G. Lavipour (eds), *Controlling Multinational Enterprises: Problems, Strategies, Counterstrategies* (Boulder: Westview Press, 1976).

24

foreign private investment and these are based on five main investing countries. Furthermore, within the groups of large firms there is a considerable concentration of investment. Fifteen firms in the United States, each with foreign assets of over $100 million, are reported to have accounted for 35 per cent of American manufacturing investment in 1957; and forty six manufacturing firms in the United Kingdom accounted for 71 per cent of all British manufacturing investment in 1962.[8]

Data on production and exports also show a similar pattern of concentration. The value added of all multinational enterprises, estimated at $500,000 million in 1971, was about one fifth of world gross national product (GNP), not including the centrally-planned economies. The value added by each of the top ten multinational enterprises was in excess of $3,000 million. Within the multinationals as a group, moreover, production was highly concentrated; of the 650 largest multinational enterprises in the manufacturing sector, the four largest accounted for 10 per cent of total sales and the 211 largest (32 per cent of the total) accounted for about 70 per cent.[9]

The significance of production abroad by multinational enterprises is also shown by the fact that the ratio of foreign production to exports for the United States is around 380 per cent and for the United Kingdom it is 202 per cent. Comparable figures for West Germany and Japan are 36 per cent and 48 per cent respectively. In the United States, estimates of the Tariff Commission, since replaced by the International Trade Commission, show that in 1970 American-based multinational enterprises accounted for 25 per cent of world exports of all commodities and about 20 per cent of world exports of manufactures. Over that period 1966-70 the growth of exports of multinational enterprises (69 per cent) exceeded that of world exports (53 per cent).

Contribution of Foreign Firms to
Developing-country Output

Data on the share of the foreign firms in the production and exports of the developing countries are sparse. A rough estimate puts the share of foreign enterprises in the total output of the developing countries at 6 per cent.[10] This statistic, however, varies enormously from country to country. In Singapore, in 1966, foreign firms are reported to have contributed one third of the total value added in manufacturing. In the 1970s foreign-controlled enterprises are reported to have accounted for 28 per cent of Mexico's manufacturing output, 31 per cent of Argentina's and 13 per cent of India's. The contribution of foreign firms to exports also shows considerable variation among the developing countries. In countries like India and Pakistan it amounts to around 10 per cent of their total exports of manufactures, whereas in countries with more open economies like Hong Kong, Taiwan and South Korea foreign firms contribute around 15 to 30 per cent of their exports of manufactures. This figure is considerably higher for Latin American countries. The share of foreign firms in the total exports of manufactures of Latin America is reported to have increased from 12 per cent in 1957 and to over 41 per cent in 1966.[11]

Related to the size, scope and sectoral composition of the activities of multinational enterprises is the dominant role they play in research-and-development activity. As discussed in the previous chapter, it is their technological capabilities that are at the heart of most explanations of multinational enterprises. In the United States, multinational enterprises account for more than 80 per cent of research-and-development expenditure in technologically-intensive industries. Twenty of the largest firms in the OECD countries, with the exception of Japan, accounted for 60 to 70 per cent of all research-and-development activity in each country over the period 1963-65.[12] The significance of the multinationals' activities in research and development is also enhanced by the fact that their expenditure on R & D, as a proportion of sales, is consistently higher in all industries in the United States than those of home-market oriented firms. For manufacturing as a whole, this figure was 230 per cent higher for the American-based multinational enterprises than for the wholly home-market oriented American firms.[13]

The above statistics, although scant in many respects, highlight the important features of foreign private investment which are of relevance to the issues raised in the context of international transfer of technology.

First, size of foreign private investment in developing countries: in absolute terms the stock of foreign private investment in developing countries is not very high. It accounted for only 30 per cent of the total stock of foreign private investment held by the market-oriented economies at the end of 1967. The developing countries, however, in 1967, accounted for only one sixth of world GNP and one fifth of world exports. Relative to these figures, a one third share in the world stock of foreign private investment is of great significance to these countries. It should also be noted that in recent years foreign private investment has accounted for nearly half of all private capital flows to the developing countries and for 26 per cent of all capital flows including official aid.[14]

Secondly, it is of significance that foreign private investment in the developing countries is concentrated in a limited number of countries.[15] Part of the explanation lies in these countries' endowments of oil and minerals. Taiwan, Singapore, Malaysia, Brazil and Mexico, however, have a considerable amount of foreign investment in their manufacturing industries. As noted earlier, the attraction of foreign private investment, especially in the manufacturing sector, to these countries is to be explained for most part by their policies towards foreign private investment and the 'climate' they provide for the operations of foreign firms.

Thirdly, recent trends show the increasing attraction of the manufacturing sector to foreign firms with an emphasis on skill-intensive industries such as chemicals, machinery and transport equipment.[16] Much of the recent debate on foreign private investment relates to the manufacturing sector. It is in the context of foreign manufacturing investment that issues relating to the inappropriateness of imported technology and the viability of technology-transmission mechanisms, other than foreign private investment, are discussed.

Fourthly, the concentration of foreign investment and research-and-development activity in a limited number of firms poses crucial issues relating to the bargaining strength of the developing countries *vis-à-vis* multinational enterprises such as the pricing of imported technologies and the 'technological dependence' of the developing countries.

Finally, the importance of the recent increase in foreign private investment by countries, other than the United States and the United Kingdom, is to be noted. An examination of the ratio of the annual increase of foreign-investment flows to the GDP of the investing countries, suggests that Japan and West Germany are internationalising their production facilities at the same rate as the United States.[17] Considering the potential of their economies, Japan and West Germany appear to be at the threshold of a significant internalisation of their production. An important and related fact is the recent tendency of American-based multinational enterprises to direct increasingly their attention to Africa and Asia. During the period 1961 to 1971, only 56 per cent of new United States affiliates in manufacturing in the developing countries were located in Latin America—their traditional stronghold; the remainder were located in Africa, Asia and Oceania.[18] These trends are significant in so far as they point to increasing competition among the source countries for the markets in the developing countries, which may reduce the developing countries' dependence on any one source for their capital and technological needs.

NOTES AND REFERENCES

1.See Charles P. Kindleberger, *American Business Abroad: Six Lectures on Direct Investment* (New Haven: Yale University Press, 1969).

2.Richard E. Caves, 'International Corporations: the Industrial Economics of Foreign Investment', *Economica*, London, February 1971.

3.Vernon, 'International Investment and International Trade in the Product Cycle', *Quarterly Journal of Economics*, Cambridge, Massachusetts, May 1966. Also see Vernon, *Sovereignty at Bay*, *op. cit.*

4.Peter Buckley and Mark Casson, *The Future of the Multinational Enterprise* (London: Macmillan, 1976) Ch. 2.

5.Stephen P. Magee, 'Multinational Corporations, the Industry Technology Cycle and Development', *Journal of World Trade Law*, London, July-August 1977, p. 301.

6.Buckley and Casson, *op. cit.*, pp. 38-9.

7.See G. K. Helleiner, 'Manufactured Exports from Less Developed Countries and Multinational Firms', *Economic Journal*, Cambridge, March 1973.

8.Stephen Hymer and Robert Rowthorn, 'Multinational Corporations and International Oligopoly: the Non-American Challenge', in Kindleberger (ed.), *The International Corporation* (Cambridge, Massachusetts: MIT Press, 1970).

9.*Multinational Corporations in World Development* (New York: United Nations, 1973) p. 13 and Table 1.

10.Grant L. Reuber *et al.*, *Private Foreign Investment in Development* (Oxford: Clarendon Press, 1973) p. 4.

11.*Multinational Corporations in World Development, op. cit.*, p. 21.

12.*Gaps in Technology: Analytical Report* (Paris: OECD Secretariat, 1968).

13.Buckley and Casson, *op. cit.*, pp. 24-5.

14.*Development Corporation, 1976 Review* (Paris: OECD Secretariat, 1976) Table 16.

15.The OECD Review, cited above, draws attention to the tendency of foreign private investment to concentrate on the rich developing countries. At the end of 1974, 61 per cent of foreign private investment is reported to have been in countries with a per capita GNP of $700 and above. Most of these countries are endowed with either petroleum or mineral resources.

16.In India, for instance, the share of the manufacturing sector in total foreign private investment is reported to have increased from 27.8 per cent in 1948 to 64.2 per cent at the end of 1972. Plantations and mining which together accounted for 25 per cent of the total stock of investment in 1948 accounted for only 15.6 per cent at the end of 1972 (*Reserve Bank of India Bulletin*, various issues).

17.Bernard Mennis and Karl P. Sauvant, *Emerging Forms of Transnational Community* (Lexington: Lexington Books, 1976) p. 15.

18.*Ibid.*, p. 11.

CHAPTER THREE

Characteristics of the Market
for Technology

WHILE foreign private investment is generally acknowledged to be a major conduit for the international transfer
of technology, grave concern is often expressed about the
costs, terms and conditions on which it is transferred. The
call for 'fair commercial practices', and the need for
access to modern technology on favourable terms in the
NIEO declaration, reflected this concern. This is also a
major theme in the studies on technology transfers by
the United Nations Conference on Trade and Development (UNCTAD).[1] It is argued that the prices charged
for imported technologies are 'excessive', foreign firms
earn relatively high rates of return on capital, the out-
flows of foreign exchange in the form of dividends and
royalty payments exceed inflows of foreign private capital
and foreign firms engage in transfer-pricing practices as a
method of avoiding taxes.

The empirical evidence cited in support of these
arguments is weak. There is no appreciable difference in
the rates of return earned by American-based multinational enterprises on their investments in the developed
and developing countries. That some foreign firms engage
in the practice of transfer-pricing cannot be denied. But
the extent of such practices is not likely to be high.

Yet this concern regarding the 'over-pricing' of
technology by foreign firms is not entirely unjustified. As
reported in the previous chapter, the bulk of foreign

30

private investment and technology is accounted for by a limited number of multinational enterprises. Given the oligopolistic and highly imperfect nature of the market for technology, there is bound to be an element of monopoly in the pricing of technology. The crucial issues, however, relate to the extent of such over-pricing and the possible remedies.

Is Knowledge a Free Good?

The criticism that the multinationals earn exorbitantly high profits is often based on a vague understanding of the theoretical point that knowledge displays the characteristics of a 'free good'. It is a free good in the sense that the use of it does not diminish its stock and it cannot be appropriated by individuals. In theory the marginal cost of replicating an existing invention is trivial compared to the average cost of research and development. If it were sold on the open market it would become freely available as it can be reproduced at little or no cost. It follows that in order to maximise the social benefits arising from the production of knowledge it should be freely transmitted without limit rather than monopolising it and charging for it.[2] The resentment of the high profits earned by multinational enterprises is in part based on the thesis that they have monopolised what ought to be a free good.

This thesis, however, ignores the question of how the motivation for further production of knowledge is to be preserved. If the firms engaging in research and development cannot appropriate the rents from such activity, the future flows of knowledge would diminish. The private rate of return from the production of knowledge being lower than the social rate of return, profit-maximising firms would have no incentive to invest in its production. 'Appropriability', or the ability of the firm to garner to itself the rents flowing from its investments in the production of knowledge, is a problem widely discussed in the literature on the economies of information and knowledge.[3]

The ideal solution to the problem would be socialisation of knowledge; the state should invest in the creation of knowledge and distribute it freely to private markets. As Kenneth Arrow, the American economist, puts it, 'in an ideal socialist economy, the reward for invention would be completely separated from any charge to the users of information'.[4] This, though, is a theoretical ideal. In any case, a great deal of basic research is funded by the state in many countries and is conducted in universities and non-profit making research institutes.

The adaptation of this knowledge to industrial and commercial usage or 'applied research' is an activity conducted mostly by private firms. By its very nature, applied research cannot often be divested from the business of manufacturing and marketing. As long as market-oriented economies depend on private firms for the generation and dissemination of knowledge in commercial usage, mechanisms for the preservation of incentives for continued production of such knowledge are needed. The patent system is in fact one such device. This is also the reason for the attempts made by private firms to preserve their monopoly over technology. Indeed, as pointed out in the previous chapter, the evolution of the multinational enterprise is to be traced to their attempts to overcome the problem of appropriability. It is the desire to internalise the externalities in the market for knowledge; and the need to appropriate the rent from their investments in research and development on the part of the foreign firms that explains the spread of multinational enterprises. The costs of appropriation tend to be lower in oligopolies and monopolies and it encourages research and development.

Much, if not all, of the monopoly profits earned by foreign firms may thus merely reflect the fact that they are appropriating returns to their past investments in

32

research and development. Such investments do not appear in the books of the foreign firms as additions to material capital. This tends to understate the capital base on which the rates of return are estimated, resulting in the misleading impression that the rates of return earned by foreign firms are disproportionately high.

COST OF TRANSFER OF TECHNOLOGY

Much of the criticism of 'over-pricing' of technologies also ignores the organisational problems associated with technology transfers. It would be misleading to think of the market for technology in terms of a market where goods are bought and sold. The oft repeated thesis that the marginal cost of transferring technology is zero is somewhat of an exaggeration. It could be so if technology transfers were limited to the transfer of blue-prints and designs. The crux of technology transfer, however, is that it not only includes knowledge embodied in blue-prints and designs, but also the transmission of human skills and information required to make the embodied technology operative.

The resource cost of transferring such technology could be considerable. It was recently reported that in a sample of twenty six transfer projects relating to chemicals, petroleum-refining and machinery industries, transfer costs were in the range of 2 to 50 per cent of the total costs of projects, with an average for all the projects at around 19 per cent. This variation between projects is accounted for by differences in the nature of the technology transferred, the age of the technology, the transferor firm's experience and the absorptive capacity of the recipient firm.[5]

DEVELOPING COUNTRIES' SHARE OF THE BURDEN

The gist of the foregoing discussion is that society has to pay for the promotion of research and development and the production of new knowledge. It could be argued, even so, that the developing countries have been forced to bear a disproportionate share of the burden. Whether or not this is so is a contentious issue. The thesis that they do bear a higher share of the burden has several strands bearing on the issues of discriminatory pricing policies of the foreign firms, transfer-pricing and the costs of patents.

Harry G. Johnson argued that in fact the developing countries are getting their technology relatively cheap. His argument was that because of their low income levels developing countries have a relatively elastic demand for imported technologies. And foreign firms, in their attempts to extract the highest possible returns from each individual buyer, act as discriminating monopolists and charge the developing countries a lower price than what they charge the others.[6] Others, though, have argued that because of their lack of bargaining power, and the absence of information about alternative streams and sources of technologies available, the developing countries strike a poor bargain.

The available evidence is not sufficient to settle the issue. It is, however, an acknowledged fact that the market for technology is highly imperfect. A major cause of this imperfection is the lack of information on the part of the purchasers about the products they are buying. As Constantine Vaitsos, the Colombian economist, put it, 'the item itself that one needs to purchase is at the same time the information that is needed in order to make a rational decision to buy it. What is needed is knowledge about knowledge.'[7] This is one of the principal reasons for the element of 'monopoly' present in the prices charged for imported technology. Clearly what is required in such cases is the provision of a greater flow of information to purchasers about alternative sources and streams of technologies.

One other reason for the element of 'monopoly' in the profits made by foreign firms has so often been cited that it hardly needs emphasising. It is that the import-substituting industrialisation policies followed by most developing countries have afforded heavy protection to the foreign-based firms; and the element of monopoly present in their profits is a reflection of this protection. In such cases the obvious remedy is to promote competition by following outward-looking policies and lowering the degree of protection to the foreign-based firms.[8]

PROBLEM OF TRANSFER-PRICING

An important facet of the multinational enterprise, discussed in Chapter 2 of this essay, is the internalisation of operations. Many of the transactions in technology, services and commodities between countries now take place between different units of the same enterprise rather than through external markets. It is the valuation placed on these transactions that has been a vexed issue in discussions of foreign private investment. As these transactions are under the control of the enterprise the prices charged for them could differ substantially from those that would be obtained in 'arm's length' transactions. They can, therefore, be manipulated to shift profits from one area of operations to another, depriving governments of their share of tax revenues. This is what UNCTAD refers to as 'hidden costs' of technology imports and what is now known as the problem of transfer-pricing.

There are a number of motives for transfer-pricing which can all be grouped under two heads: profit-maximisation and risk-minimisation. Under the profit-maximisation motive, the incentives for transfer-pricing arise from international differences in tax and tariff rates, foreign-exchange restrictions in the host countries on profit remittances, exchange-rate instability and regulations on royalty rates and technical-fee payments, as well as the existence of local shareholders. Under the risk-minimisation motive, the incentives for transfer-pricing arise from anticipated balance-of-payments problems, threats of impending nationalisation, trade-union pressures and the need to keep a low-profit profile in the host countries.[9]

In theory, the main fiscal incentive for transfer-pricing arises from tax-rate and tariff-rate differentials between countries. The firm will find it advantageous to over-price its exports to its subsidiaries if the host-country tariff rate is smaller than the tax advantage of declaring profits in the home country (resulting from the difference between the home and host country tax rates). It would find it advantageous to under-price its exports if the host-country tariff-rate is bigger than the tax advantage to be obtained by declaring profits at home.

The understanding of the motivation for transfer-pricing is, however, not matched by adequate empirical evidence. The bulk of the evidence relates to the problem of glaring excesses in the pharmaceutical industry—a problem acutely felt both by the developed and developing countries. Sanjaya Lall, of Oxford University, shows that over-pricing in the foreign-owned pharmaceutical firms in Colombia ranged from 33 per cent to more than 300 per cent of international market prices during the years 1966-70. Similarly, Professor Vaitsos has reported over-pricing of pharmaecutical products averaging 155 per cent, rubber industry averaging 40 per cent, chemicals 25.5 per cent and electronics industry in the range of 16 to 60 per cent. These estimates relate to Colombia for the year 1968.[10]

Two points of significance emerge out of the available empirical evidence. First, the incidence of transfer-pricing appears to be high only in the technologically-intensive industries such as pharmaceuticals. Secondly, George Kopitz, of the International Monetary Fund (IMF), in an extensive survey, suggests that the influence of tax-rate differentials on transfer prices is not borne out by empirical evidence.[11]

36

The principal motivation for transfer-pricing, therefore, appears to be non-fiscal incentives, especially ceilings on profit repatriation, royalty rates and technical fees imposed by the host countries. The Colombian evidence also suggests that the existence of governmental ceilings on profit remissions by subsidiaries from Colombia may have been a major incentive for transfer-pricing. The implication of this is that the attempts by the governments of host countries to limit the amount of profits taken by the multinational enterprises may affect the form in which profits are taken—but not their size.[12]

Lack of empirical evidence on the extent of transfer-pricing does not, however, amount to saying that the problem does not exist. In any case, the potential for transfer-pricing could be substantial. Sidney Robbins and Robert Stobaugh, for instance, have estimated in a recent book that a 10 per cent change in the estimated $40,000 million intra-firm sales by all American-based multinational enterprises in 1972 would have exceeded all receipts of royalties and management fees and would approximate the size of dividend payments.[13] The actual use of transfer-pricing may be substantially below this potential, but it suggests that the problem is real.

SOLUTIONS TO THE TRANSFER-PRICING PROBLEM

Several remedial measures may be suggested to overcome this problem.

First, is the need to establish meaningful and consistent arm's-length prices for valuing the intra-firm transactions of the multinationals. This would require inter-governmental cooperation in the sharing of information. The efforts of the Brussels Customs Cooperation Council in pooling information on the customs evaluation of imported goods by the signatories to the Brussels Valuation Convention may be a pointer in this direction. It would also require the coordination of effort among different tax authorities in the host countries, who may be often working at cross purposes. Tariff and tax rates could be fixed in such a way that the revenue realised would be the same whether the multinational enterprise transmits profits by over-pricing imports or by declaring its profits.[14]

Secondly, the host countries may have to weigh the advantages of imposing ceilings on remittances of dividends, royalties and fees, against the losses they incur by way of transfer-pricing. The empirical evidence suggests that such restrictions are more the cause of transfer-pricing than tax differentials, so it may be in the interests of developing countries to relax such regulations and tighten their fiscal surveillance. To the extent that the transfer-pricing problem arises from the risk-minimisation motive of the foreign firms, an improvement in the political and economic climate for their operations should go a long way to alleviate the problem.

Thirdly, far-reaching fiscal policy innovations have also been proposed to remedy the problem. Host-government taxation of the multinational enterprises, on the basis of their global profits allocated to a particular country by using a formula based on their sales or capital accounted for by the country in question, is one such. Another is the taxation of the global profits of the foreign firms jointly by all the countries in which they operate and the sharing of the proceeds. These solutions, however, pose insuperable problems of administration, co-ordination and harmonisation, not only in levying the taxes but also in sharing the proceeds. In the final analysis, the most practicable remedies belong to the sphere of coordination of information, improvements in the bargaining strength and fiscal surveillance of the developing countries. It is in these areas that international action and inter-governmental cooperation are required.

PATENTS: NON-PROBLEM

The role of the patent system in the market for technology has been the subject of debate for a long time. It has, however, come under heavy fire in recent years in the context of international transfer of technology to developing countries. The main criticisms of the patent system are that (i) it accentuates the imperfections in the market for technology, (ii) strengthens the monopoly of foreign firms over technology and product markets and (iii) it does little or nothing to promote research and development in the developing countries. The factual basis for these criticisms is that the bulk of the patents in existence, including those granted by the developing countries, are owned by foreign firms. Most of these patents are not worked in the developing countries and the sale of patent-embodied technology is often hemmed in by various restriction clauses.[15]

While there is a modicum of truth in all these, it must be noted that much of these criticisms are generic to the very institution of the patent system. The dilemma the system poses is that while it is needed to encourage the production of new knowledge it limits the free flow of such knowledge. Most proposals, including those that advocate its abolition, are rooted in this dilemma. This problem, however, may not be any more acute in the developing countries than it is in the developed countries. Critics, nevertheless, attach special significance to the heavy concentration of patents in the hands of the foreign firms operating in the developing countries, the failure of those firms to work much of these patents and the restrictions imposed on the sale of patent-embodied technology.

The thrust of these criticisms is directed at showing that prices paid for the imports of patented products are excessive, the non-use of patents by foreign firms precludes local production and that patented technology is overpriced. These arguments, however, can be overdrawn. The limitations of these arguments have been shown in a penetrating article by Sanjaya Lall.[16] First, it has to be established that the prices paid for imports of patented products are higher than they would have been in the absence of patents or that there are alternative sources of cheaper imports. Secondly, the argument that the non-use of patents by foreign firms prevents local production assumes that such local production is beneficial on economic grounds and that it is actually prevented by the patent holders. If local production is neither economical nor likely to be undertaken by local producers the costs of non-use of patents may not amount to much. Thirdly, the restrictive clauses imposed by foreign firms, though they may be undesirable, cannot all be traced to patents. They are also found in sales of non-patented technology.

It should be noted, too, that multinational enterprises may have more important sources of monopoly power than patents. The very complexity of modern technology, the importance of scale economies in research and development and the increasing importance of marketing skills may be more important to the multinationals in preserving their monopoly over technology than patents. As Sanjaya Lall notes, many industries, with the exception of pharmaceuticals, do not seem to bother with patents at all.

On balance, therefore, too much seems to be made of the costs of patents than is warranted. In fact the developing countries may derive some positive benefits by going along with the patent system. As Edith Penrose, of the European Institute of Business Administration (INSEAD), Fontainebleau, succinctly puts it, 'given the existence of national patent systems, and given the interests, motives and policies of multinational firms, which are the chief international investors, it may be that cooperation in this system on the part of the less developed countries will help them to obtain the cooperation of such firms in introducing and developing new technology'.[17]

The conclusions of this section can be summarised thus: the criticisms relating to the over-pricing of technologies are not wholly unfounded. It would, however, be an exaggeration to say that the profits made by the foreign firms are disproportionately high in relation to the costs of production and transmission of knowledge. This is a misconception arising from a vague understanding of the nature of the market for knowledge. The element of monopoly in the operation of foreign firms for the most part arises from developing countries' lack of information on the sources and streams of technology, their lack of bargaining strength and their protectionist policies. The problem of transfer-pricing, in spite of lack of adequate empirical evidence, cannot be lightly dismissed. Here again, much of the incentives for such practices appear to arise from the risk-minimisation motive. The attitudes of developing countries towards foreign-enterprise participation could have a significant impact on transfer-pricing. The problem could be mitigated, if not wholly overcome, by international action in the dissemination of information on arm's-length prices and joint action by the developing countries. The costs of the patent system appear to be over-emphasised.

NOTES AND REFERENCES

1.*Major Issues Arising from the Transfer of Technology to Developing Countries* (Geneva: UNCTAD Secretariat, 1975).

2.For a lucid discussion of this point see Harry G. Johnson, 'The Efficiency and Welfare Implications of the Multinational Corporation', in Kindleberger (ed.), *The Multinational Corporation*, *op. cit.*, pp. 35-6.

3.See Kenneth J. Arrow, 'Economic Welfare and the Allocation of Resources for Invention', in *The Rate and Director of Inventive Activity: Economic and Social Considerations* (Princeton, New Jersey: Princeton University Press, for the National Bureau of Economic Research, 1962).

4.*Ibid.*, p. 617.

5.David J. Teece, 'Technology Transfer by Multinational Firms: the Resource Cost of Transferring Technological Know-how', *Economic Journal*, June 1977.

6.Johnson, *op. cit.*

7.Constantine Vaitsos, *Transfer of Resources and Preservation of Monopoly Rents* (Cambridge, Massachusetts: Havard University Press, 1970) p. 28.

8.For a detailed discussion of this point, see MacBean and Balasubramanyam, *op. cit.*, Ch. 8.

9.For a lucid discussion of motivation see Sanjaya Lall, 'Transfer Pricing by Multinational Manufacturing Firms', *Oxford Bulletin of Economics and Statistics*, August 1973, pp. 173-95; and George F. Kopitz, 'Taxation and Multinational Firm Behaviour', *IMF Staff Papers*, Washington, November 1976, pp. 652-9.

10.Lall, *op. cit.*, and Vaitsos, *Inter-country Income Distributions and Trans-national Enterprises* (Oxford: Clarendon Press, 1974) p. 47.

11.Kopitz, *op. cit.*

12.See Vernon, *Sovereignty at Bay, op. cit.*, pp. 139-40.

13.Sidney Robbins and Robert B. Stobaugh, *Money in the Multinational Enterprise: a Study in Financial Policy* (London: Longmans, 1974) p. 92.

14.See Corden, 'The Theory of International Trade', in Dunning (ed.), *Economic Analysis and the Multinational Enterprise* (London: Allen & Unwin, 1974) p. 204.

15.Vaitsos, 'Patents Revisited: their Functions in Developing Countries', *Journal of Development Studies*, London, October 1972, pp. 71-91; and *The Role of Patents in the Transfer of Technology of Developing Countries* (New York: United Nations, 1964).

16.Lall, 'The Patent System and the Transfer of Technology to Less-Developed Countries', *Journal of World Trade Law*, London, January-February 1976, pp. 1-16.

17.Edith T. Penrose, 'International Patenting and Developing Countries', *Economic Journal*, September 1973, p. 785.

CHAPTER FOUR

Inappropriateness of Imported Technologies

A FREQUENT criticism of imported technologies is that they tend to be capital-intensive and are inappropriate to the needs of labour-rich and capital-poor developing countries. This, in fact, is one of the major planks of the thesis that technological dependence is the root cause of underdevelopment. It has provided the critics with a convenient peg on which to hang many of the problems faced by the developing countries on the foreign firms.

A proximate cause of unemployment and mal-distribution is seen to arise from the import of capital-intensive technologies. The usual riposte to this argument is that the capital intensity of foreign firms is influenced by factor-price distortions in the factor markets of the developing countries. Due to various institutional factors, the market price of labour tends to be overstated, relative to its true opportunity costs, while that of capital is understated. Profit-maximising firms respond to these market prices and adopt capital-intensive techniques of production. More recent conceptions of the 'inappropriateness' thesis, however, also blame the foreign firms for factor-price distortions. They have access to international capital markets where capital is relatively cheap and they pay high-wage rates, based on international standards, for not only skilled labour and management but also for unskilled labour. Factor-market distortions are therefore a consequence of the operations of foreign firms. Such distortions also encourage local firms to adopt capital-intensive techniques.[1]

These arguments concerning 'inappropriateness' of imported technologies are reinforced by the 'inappropriate-product' argument. The products manufactured by foreign firms embody characteristics which are often excessively sophisticated and superfluous in relation to the income levels and needs of the developing countries. These products by their very nature embody capital-intensive techniques. Such products are associated with highly imperfect oligopolistic markets where advertising and marketing skills play a crucial role. The appearance of such new products displaces the old ones in the market —the ones embodying low-income characteristics—with deleterious effects on employment and the distribution of incomes.

CAPITAL INTENSITY

Central to the thesis of 'inappropriateness' is the argument that the techniques adopted by foreign firms are those perfected in response to the factor endowments of developed countries. They are therefore invariably capital-intensive and foreign firms fail to adopt labour-intensive techniques even when they are available. Another strand of the thesis is that multinational enterprises operate in industries typified by technological 'fixity' in the sense of the elasticity of factor-substitution being low.

These arguments mostly rest on casual empiricism based on observations of the operations of foreign firms at the aggregate manufacturing sector level. Recent empirical studies at the disaggregated industry level bring these generalisations into dispute. Frequently the operations of foreign firms are shown to be less capital-intensive than those of locally-owned firms in the same industry groups. Howard Pack, in a recent study of factor proportions in forty two plants in the Kenyan manufacturing sector

44

relating to food processing, paints, chemicals, textiles and plastic containers, found that foreign-owned firms were relatively less capital-intensive than locally-owned firms. It is of significance that Dr Pack attributes this phenomenon more to the technical perception and managerial expertise of foreign firms in identifying the existence of labour-intensive techniques and organising them than to the influence of factor-prices.[2]

Similar findings are also reported by an International Labour Organisation (ILO) employment mission to Kenya. In a comparison of foreign and locally-owned firms in similar industrial sections, it was found that the former were 20 to 30 per cent less capital-intensive than the latter. Again the ILO mission attributes the lower capital-intensity of foreign firms to their superior skills in the organisation and supervision of labour.[3]

The thesis of technical 'fixity' does not also appear to survive empirical tests. Statistical studies, both in the developed and developing countries, show that sectoral elasticities of substitution are significantly different from zero and range between 0.5 to 1.6.[4] Foreign firms, as several studies show, have not been slow in seizing available opportunities to substitute labour for capital. Such substitution has not only occurred in anciliary activities (handling, packaging, sorting out spare parts, internal transportation *et cetera*), but also in the production process itself, through adaptation of machinery, use of increased shifts, greater machine speeds and sub-contracting of selected production processes.[5]

TECHNOLOGICAL CHOICE

The available empirical evidence, though not comprehensive, brings into dispute the assumption that foreign firms are invariably capital-intensive in their operations and that they choose not to adopt labour-intensive techniques even when they exist.

Yet it is true that at the aggregate manufacturing-sector level the capital intensity of foreign firms tends to be high and they have not shown any excessive enthusiasm for adding to the stock of labour-intensive techniques. Reasons for this are to be sought in the developing countries' economic policies, their attitudes towards technological borrowing and foreign private investment and the nature of the market for technology.

A frequently-cited reason for the adoption of capital-intensive techniques by foreign firms is the incentive to do so provided by the import-substituting industrialisation policies followed by most developing countries. The tariffs and quotas imposed on imports designed to facilitate import-substituting industrialisation provides the foreign firms with highly profitable domestic markets sheltered from international competition. In the absence of effective price competition, the foreign firms have no incentive to adopt socially-efficient, labour-intensive techniques. Instead, they follow the path of least resistance: the adoption of capital-intensive techniques tested and tried abroad. When the firms have a monopolistic advantage in the product markets, there is less pressure on them to minimise costs—the objective of the so-called 'economic man'. And the objective of the 'engineering man', to push the production process towards more advanced automated techniques, prevails. This, of course, applies equally to foreign and local firms.[6] Indeed, most developing countries, in their bid for speedy industrialisation, have provided positive incentives to the foreign firms to adopt capital-intensive techniques such as generous depreciation allowances, lower tax rates for designated industries, tax holidays for new and 'priority' industries and concessionary tariff rates on imports of machinery and equipment.

The drive towards capital intensity is also influenced by many other factors not usually perceived in standard discussions of the issue. Motives of risk-minimisation on the part of entrepreneurs, the preference for the latest

46

and modern techniques on the part of businessmen and governments in the developing countries and the non-availability of skilled personnel to supervise labour-intensive techniques are some of these. Capital-intensive techniques, although they may entail higher unit costs of production, allow the entrepreneurs to respond quickly to unexpected fluctuations in demand. The preference for 'modern' techniques on the part of the developing countries has long been noted. In fact the NIEO declaration called for access to modern technologies on the part of the developing countries.

A major reason for the lack of enthusiasm on the part of foreign firms to add to the stock of labour-intensive technologies is related to the problem of appropriability, discussed in the previous chapter, as it tends to be low in the case of labour-intensive technologies relative to capital-intensive technologies. Not only can the former be more easily imitated but their adoption would also reduce the profits of the firm on its more sophisticated technologies. It is thus that foreign firms have little incentive to invest in the production of labour-intensive technologies. 'Feedback' clauses found in technology-licensing agreements, requiring purchasers of technology to make available to the seller, free of charge, any improvements and adaptations they make, are also a device to overcome the problem of appropriability.[7]

POLICIES TO PROMOTE LABOUR-INTENSIVE TECHNIQUES

While there are valid reasons to argue that the operations of foreign firms tend to be capital-intensive, not all of the problem can be traced to their 'foreignness'. The available empirical evidence shows that in the presence of incentives to adopt labour-intensive technologies they have done so. For the most part, such incentives appear to have been limited. In fact, the policies of developing countries designed to attract inflows of foreign private capital, such as generous depreciation allowances, tax holidays and other fiscal incentives, may have provided a positive inducement to the foreign firms to adopt capital-intensive technologies. As has so often been advocated in recent years, policies directed at subsidising labour rather than capital may have some impact on the choice of techniques by the foreign firms. Such policies may, however, be of limited significance. More important may be the need to increase the degree of effective competition in the product markets.

The above analysis shows that the adoption of capital-intensive technologies, even if their unit costs of production are high, tends to be high in monopolistic structures. The high profits provided by the monopolistic markets more than offset the need to minimise costs. If the 'economic man', with his objective of minimising costs, is to prevail over the 'engineering man', product markets need to be made more competitive. If domestic markets do not provide sufficient opportunities to do so, we may have to look to the international markets to provide such competition. This would imply encouraging production for export. Multinational enterprises are already playing a significant role in the exports of manufactures from developing countries. Although not all manufacturing for exports may be based on labour-intensive techniques, it is the presumption that, faced with international competition, foreign firms would seek cost-minimising efficient techniques. These tend to be at the labour-intensive end of the spectrum.

This solution, however, is not without its problems. It is likely that exports of manufactures from the developing countries will be increasingly subject to restrictions imposed by the importing countries. Moreover, manufacturing for export may place the developing countries in a weak bargaining position, since they would have neither a monopoly over scarce resources nor control over the markets they serve. A major benefit from such activity, however, would be the employment it creates. This could be a substantial gain for countries suffering from serious unemployment problems. The subject of exports of manufactures from the developing countries produced under the aegis of multinational enterprises is in need of much more analysis and research than it has so far received.

It is also likely that the removal of tariffs and quotas on imports may reduce the inflows of foreign capital into many of the developing countries. The likely benefits, in terms of employment creation, however, arising from a pursuit of 'outward-looking' policies needs to be weighed against the losses arising out of reduced inflows of foreign private capital. Moreover, it is doubtful if protectionist policies have had as strong an influence on imports of foreign private capital as is often claimed. It is the 'climate' for foreign private investments in terms of infra-structure, exchange-rate stability and a liberal attitude towards free enterprise in general that may be more important in attracting foreign private capital than protectionist policies.

Exposing foreign firms to international competition by encouraging exports is only one method of increasing the degree of competition in a bid to promote their adoption of 'efficient' labour-intensive technologies. Forces of competition in the domestic market, often hampered by domestic industrial licensing policies and other regulations, also need to be encouraged. Furthermore, a more liberal attitude towards imports of foreign private capital and technology should encourage competition among the suppliers of technology, especially in view of the increasing importance of 'new' entrants such as Japan and West Germany in the international market for technology.

In so far as 'appropriability' is the problem limiting the production of labour-intensive technologies by the foreign firms, legal guarantees providing them with temporal monopolies over such technologies may have to be provided. One such device, already in operation in some developed countries, endorsed by Professor Magee, is the 'Utility Model'.[8] A 'Utility Model' is a simple patent, of short duration, easier to obtain than the traditional patents and applies to both products and processes.[9] The restriction clauses found in technology-licensing agreements, referred to earlier, are also a device to overcome the appropriability problem. While there may be good grounds for advocating their elimination, it must be recognised that such elimination may result in a reduction in the amount of knowledge produced in future.

INAPPROPRIATE PRODUCTS

A common criticism of multinational enterprises is that the products they produce cater mainly to the needs of the upper-income groups in developing countries and that such production results in a misallocation of resources. This criticism is usually met by arguing that it is the skewed-income distribution patterns in developing countries that generate a demand for such products; and the production of such products by multinational enterprises is no more than a rational response of profit-maximising firms to the dictates of the market. The ideal solution to the problem is to correct the income-distribution pattern which gives rise to a demand for such products.

Recent conceptions of 'inappropriateness', however, are much stronger in their criticism of the production patterns of multinational enterprises. They include the whole range of consumer goods produced by multinationals in their definition of 'inappropriateness'. The appearance of 'new' products embodying sophisticated characteristics and capital-intensive technologies displace the old products on the market. Partly because of the disappearance of old products and partly because some of the new products are sufficiently inexpensive to be possibilities for the low-income groups, consumption

50

patterns in the developing countries are imbalanced. They are imbalanced in the sense that by spending too much on the new products the low-income groups are left with insufficient incomes to spend on other goods and necessities. Furthermore, it is the production of sophisticated products embodying skilled labour and capital-intensive technologies that promotes income inequalities, which in turn provides a demand for such products.[10]

This thesis, although it has its merits, may have been overdrawn, especially in the context of some of the policies that its proponents have advocated. The advocacy of the need to search for alternative appropriate technologies is for the most part based on this thesis. In addition, an important corollary of this thesis is that by altering consumption patterns in favour of 'appropriate' products, the choice of factor proportions can be influenced in favour of labour-intensive technologies.

The so-called 'appropriate' products, according to this thesis, are those which are less sophisticated and embody low-income characteristics relative to those produced by the foreign firms. Drawing upon the 'new' approach to demand theory,[11] it is argued that consumer demand is for the need-fulfilling characteristics embodied in the product and not the product itself. If products are defined according to their ability to fulfil needs, and not on the basis of their physical characteristics, a number of seemingly disparate products can be substitutes for one another in consumption, in the sense that they all fulfil the same basic need. Thus Coca Cola, Scotch whisky and water can all be substitutes for one another, in the sense that they can all quench thirst. The products produced by the foreign firms are in response to the needs of the consumers in the developed countries. They embody sophisticated characteristics in terms of high standards of quality, labour-saving potential, attractive packaging *et cetera*, which may be relevant to the needs of the consumers in the developed countries, but are superfluous to the needs of the consumers and they can be fulfilled by less sophisticated products, embodying low-income characteristics and labour-intensive technologies.

Admittedly, the scope for satisfying a basic need by a number of different commodities is much higher than usually recognised in standard discussions on the theory of consumption. The more broadly a need is defined, the greater the number of products that can satisfy it. But the problem arises in determining the needs of the consumers. It is the presumption of the economist that consumer sovereignty exercised in the market place reflects consumer need. The critics, however, argue that due to various market imperfections, including advertising and consumer ignorance, market valuation of products is not an infallible guide to the needs of the consumer. They would be justified in advocating policies to promote consumer education which would include the provision of better information and also the regulation of advertising and promotional measures of multinational enterprises. But to go beyond that and argue that the consumers in developing countries should stick to products embodying low-income characteristics amounts to a value judgment. Moreover, such an argument also ignores dynamic considerations such as consumer learning and a drive to modernity. In any case, it is highly illogical to argue that 'it is inappropriate for developing countries to consume those goods that the developed countries produce, and inappropriate for developing countries to produce those goods which the developed countries consume'.[12]

APPROPRIATE PRODUCTS AND TECHNOLOGIES

Much more basic to the issue of choice of techniques is the inter-relationship between products and processes, the thesis postulates. It is argued that 'appropriate' products, defined as those embodying low-income characteristics, also embody 'appropriate' technologies—meaning labour-intensive technologies. There is, however, no presumption that all appropriate products necessarily embody 'labour-intensive' technologies. Examples of appropriate products embodying labour-intensive technologies are few and far between. The available empirical evidence is insufficient to generalise on the nature of the inter-relationship between products and technologies.

The description 'appropriate' often attached to labour-intensive technologies is also misleading. To the proponents of the thesis, 'appropriate' seems to convey no more than the employment potential of labour-intensive technologies. They seem to have, for the most part, ignored dynamic considerations such as efficiency and growth. While the employment potential of labour-intensive technologies may be high, they have often been found to compare poorly with capital-intensive technologies, in terms of their efficiency and the surplus they generate for future investment. In many cases they have been found to use not only more labour but also more capital per unit of output than capital-intensive technologies.[13]

It could, however, be argued that equity rather than efficiency ought to be the prime consideration in determining what is an 'appropriate' technology. The advocates of labour-intensive technologies, in fact, appear to argue that such technologies are appropriate as they have an acceptable impact on income distribution. But this may be a narrow approach to the income-distribution problem. A broader approach to the problem would consist of adopting efficient modern technologies with a higher level of output; and the redistribution of this higher level of output, by fiscal means, to compensate those who do not receive a share of the output as a consequence of not being employed. Such a scheme would also provide a surplus for reinvestment. Further, those who are unemployed, as a result of adopting modern technologies, could be absorbed in public projects, such as irrigation and road works, until a higher rate of growth makes it possible for them to be employed elsewhere.

The foregoing is not to be construed as an indictment of labour-intensive technologies in general. In cases where such technologies are relatively efficient they ought to be adopted. But the criterion of appropriateness should not be confined to short-term considerations of employment and income distribution alone. The comment of John P. Lewis, when at Princeton University, on the excessive enthusiasm for labour-intensive technologies, based on their immediate employment effects, on the part of its strong supporters, admirably sums up the point being made here: 'Their basic fallacy . . . is in the assumption that employment goals can ever be divorced from output and income goals. Any society, if it could rid itself of enough technique and capital, could keep every one of its ambulatory members fully employed, grubbing for roots and berries.'[14]

MANAGEMENT OF LABOUR-INTENSIVE TECHNOLOGIES

The considerable amount of managerial and administrative skills that are required for the adoption of labour-intensive technologies has not been given the attention it deserves. It has often been noted that it is the scarcity of supervisory personnel that has dissuaded many firms from adopting labour-intensive technologies. As pointed out earlier, it was the possession of such skills that accounted for the adoption of labour-intensive techniques by the foreign firms in the Kenyan manufacturing sector. The development of such skills may require substantial investment in training schemes. Indeed, one of the main benefits arising from the operations of foreign firms in the developing countries is the labour and managerial skills they provide.

Beyond these are issues concerning the organisation and investment in research and development required to add to the meagre stock of labour-intensive technologies. Most developing countries possess neither the resources nor the organisational capabilities required to generate new labour-intensive technologies. Whether or not it is a consequence of their low-income levels, the fact remains that investment in research and development in developing countries is miniscule. It is in the region of 0.2 to 0.5 per cent of GNP in most developing countries compared with a figure of 1.5 per cent reported for China. Moreover, the current research-and-development scene in most developing countries is characterised by an emphasis on basic, as opposed to applied, research by a lack of inter-action between various research projects and an absence of coordination between science and production. It is also recognised that investment in a few scientific research laboratories alone may not result in the development of 'appropriate' labour-intensive technologies. Successful innovations mostly depend on the enterprise of the businessman and they occur in the factory rather than in an isolated laboratory. Research and development can rarely be divorced from the production process itself, if it is to result in commercially-viable technologies.

In view of all these problems, there may be much to be gained by concentrating research effort on restructuring and adopting the existing stock of techniques to suit the needs of developing countries. The rate of return on such investment could be much higher than that resulting from investment in basic research to evolve alternative technologies. The multinational enterprises, with their endowment of skills and organisational abilities, given the right incentives, could play a vital role in restructuring and adapting existing techniques to the needs of the developing countries. Amartya Sen, of Oxford University, aptly sums up the point: 'The view that the past menu is basically inappropriate and we must make our own technology by looking for it, while full of healthy vigour is not always a very useful approach. To recognise that a whole lot of techniques already exist no matter what we do would seem to be not entirely a negligible thought.'[15]

This chapter has examined the arguments concerning the 'inappropriateness' of imported technologies. It is shown that while the operations of foreign firms may, in general, be capital-intensive, there is no presumption that it is invariably so. It cannot also be argued that the problem arises solely because of the 'foreignness' of foreign firms. Much of the problem can be traced to the policies followed by the developing countries. Furthermore, reasons for the lack of enthusiasm on the part of the foreign firms to add to the stock of labour-intensive technologies are to be found in the nature of the market for technology. In the presence of incentives to adopt labour-intensive technologies and legal guarantees to overcome the appropriability problem, foreign firms can be expected to show an interest in the development of socially-efficient technologies. The thesis that the products manufactured by the foreign firms are 'inappropriate' and a move towards the production of appropriate products will result in the adoption of labour-intensive technologies may have been overdrawn. This thesis appears to have paid scant attention to considerations of efficiency and growth. Moreover, the development of labour-intensive technologies should proceed in conjunction with the use of existing stock of technologies. Research and development should be directed at adapting and restructuring the existing techniques to suit the needs of the developing countries.

NOTES AND REFERENCES

1.Frances Stewart, *Technology and Under-development* (London: Macmillan, 1977) pp. 89-90.

2.Howard J. Pack, 'Substitution of Labour for Capital in Kenyan Manufacturing', *Economic Journal*, March 1976.

3.*Employment, Incomes and Equality* (Geneva: International Labour Organisation, 1972).

4.H. J. Bruton, *The Elasticity of Substitution in Developing Countries*, Research

Memorandum No. 45, Centre for Development Economics, Williams College, Williamstown, Massachusetts.

5.Gustar Ranis, 'Industrial Labour Absorption', *Economic Development and Cultural Change*, April 1973; R. Hal Mason, 'Some Observations on the Choices of Technology by Multinational Firms', *Review of Economies and Statistics*, August 1973; and G. K. Boon, 'Technological Choice in Metal Working with Special Reference to Mexico', in Ajith Bhalla (ed.), *Technology and Employment in Industry* (Geneva: ILO, 1975).

6.Louis T. Wells, Jr., 'Economic Man and Engineering Man: Choice of Technique in Low-Wage Country', *Public Policy*, Vol. XXI, 1973.

7.Magee, *op. cit.*

8.Magee, *op. cit.*

9.Magee, *op. cit.*

10.Stewart, *op. cit.*, pp. 80-1.

11.Kelvin Lancaster, 'Change and Innovation in the Technology of Consumption', *American Economic Review*, May 1966.

12.Stewart, 'Trade and Technology', in Paul Streeten (ed.), *Trade Strategies for Development* (London: Macmillan, 1973) p. 256.

13.A study comparing fertiliser production by conventional methods with that based on manure and gas plants in India showed that the capital costs of the latter far exceeded that of the former. Also total production costs per unit of output in the case of the intermediate technology were found to be higher than that in the modern technology, based on conventional methods. See R. Disney, *The Choice of Technology in the Third World Countries: a Case Study and Critique*, Discussion Papers in Economics Series A, No. 83 (Reading: University of Reading, 1970).

14.John P. Lewis, *Quiet Crisis in India* (New York: Anchor Books, 1964) p. 55.

15.Amartya K. Sen, *Employment, Technology and Development* (London: Oxford University Press, 1971) p. 12.

Unbundling the Multinational Investment Package

THE distinguishing feature of foreign private investment that sets it apart from other forms of international capital flows is that it is a package of technology, managerial skills and capital. The issue that has often surfaced in recent discussions of foreign investment is whether this package can be unbundled? The motivation to unbundle the package arises from the increasing concern about the control over operations exercised by foreign firms and the belief that the ingredients of capital and technology, provided by the foreign firms, can be bought separately and assembled more cheaply in some other way.

The developing countries have not been alone in expressing concern about the control over operations exercised by the foreign firms. But they have been the most articulate. Such concern not only stems from their fears of imperialistic exploitation, a hang-over from their past experience, but also from economic nationalism, a desire for ownership and control of the economy by domestic nationals. The advent of the multinational enterprise has intensified this concern. Its size, the monopoly over technology it possesses and its ability to move resources across countries with ease are all seen to pose a threat to the economic and political sovereignty of the host countries. The intensity of such concern is shown by recent book titles: *Invisible Empires, Silent Surrender, Coming Clash* and *Sovereignty at Bay*.

Less dramatic, but nonetheless widespread, is the concern that foreign private investment has resulted in the monopolistic exploitation of developing countries, has imposed a heavy burden on their balance of payments and, in general, has enabled the foreign firms to reap benefits far in excess of their contribution. Much of these costs are seen to arise from the packaged nature of foreign private investment. Foreign firms are able to combine several advantages they possess in one package and by selling the package as a whole they are able to reap high profits. The packaged nature of foreign private investment precludes separate evaluation of their various contributions. The total returns they earn on the whole combination of technology, capital, goods and services they provide may exceed what they could get by selling them separately.

Such considerations underlie the demand of developing countries that the foreign investment package should be unbundled. They have also prompted a search for technology-transmission mechanisms alternative to foreign private investment.

SUGGESTED ALTERNATIVES

The often-suggested alternatives are joint ventures, technical-collaboration agreements (licensing agreements) and management contracts.[1] The characteristic feature of these agreements is the absence of ownership of capital in a major way on the part of foreign firms entering into such arrangements. It is the belief of its advocates that, in the absence of ownership of capital, foreign firms would be precluded from exercising exclusive control over operations. It is hoped that such arrangements will enable developing countries to acquire the technology they need much more cheaply than under foreign private investment.

Such alternative arrangements have gained popularity in recent years in several developing countries, including

India. Over the period 1958-70, Indian firms in the manufacturing sector entered into more than 3,557 technical collaboration agreements with foreign firms. Only a small proportion of such agreements involved foreign financial participation and even in these cases the foreign firms had only a minor share in the equity.

In spite of their popularity, and the advantages claimed for them, it is open to question whether such arrangements are efficient conduits of technology transfer relative to foreign private investment. In assessing their relative merits, the absence of capital ownership and control over operations should not be the only considerations. More important is the extent and nature of knowledge transferred under the various arrangements and the ability of technology-recipient firms to absorb and, efficiently, utilise the knowledge transferred.

Extent of Knowledge Transferred

The particular institutional channel adopted for transferring technology largely determines the extent and nature of knowledge transferred. The mode of transfer adopted has significant implications for both the willingness and ability to transfer technology on the part of foreign firms. Their willingness to transfer technology is a function of the scope the various channels offer to fully capture the returns of their investment in the production of knowledge. In this respect, foreign private investment and technical-collaboration agreements are at opposite ends of the spectrum, with joint ventures occupying the middle ground. In the case of foreign private investment, the foreign firms' involvement in the operations, through asset participation and managerial control, tends to be high. As a result, the scope that such investment offers to fully capture the rents flowing from their monopoly over knowledge also tends to be high. Consequently, both the extent and the nature of knowledge transferred tend to be high in the case of foreign private investment. In other words, as 'appropriability' tends to be high, in the case of foreign private investment, the willingness of foreign firms to transfer technology also tends to be high.

By contrast to foreign private investment, the calculation of costs and benefits in the case of technical-collaboration agreements tends to be different and involves complex factors. Such agreements involve little or no capital participation on the part of foreign firms; and the returns to be had from the sale of technology take the form of royalty payments based on the technology-recipient firm's production or sales and, in some cases, an agreed technical-fee payment. As Yair Aharoni puts it in his book on foreign investment, 'when a licensing agreement is based on royalties alone, either in fixed fee or in proportion to sales, the licensor's decision process involves a weighing of different elements than when an equity investment is considered'.[2]

These other elements are to do with indirect effects that a technical transfer may have on the transferor firm, which may tend to reduce appropriability. First, the transferor firm has to take into account the possible erosion of its monopoly over technology, unless the production and transmission of knowledge on a continuous basis is central to its activity. Secondly, transmission of technology abroad may lead to competition from the technology-recipient firm in third markets. Thirdly, the returns from a technical-collaboration agreement may be ephemeral, lasting as long as the agreement is in force. In view of all these factors, it is likely that royalty payments and technical fees do not compensate fully the foreign firms for the investment they make in the production of knowledge and the assets they transfer. It is, therefore, the presumption that the extent and nature of knowledge transferred under such agreements tends to be lower than in the case of foreign private investment. In this context, the recommendation made to the Chemical Marketing Research Association in the United States is illuminating: 'If you have the necessary balance of resources, a wholly-owned subsidiary is preferable to a joint venture: if you use a joint venture secure control: but any share of ownership is better than a licensing agreement.'[3]

Joint ventures, although they fare much better in this respect, pose different sorts of problems. A joint venture is defined as one where there is the commitment, for more than a short duration, of funds, facilities and services, by two or more legally separate interests to an enterprise for their mutual benefit.[4] To the extent that the foreign firms entering into such ventures have a financial stake, the extent of their technical involvement can be expected to be higher than in the case of technical-collaboration agreements.

They pose, however, two sorts of problems. First, there may arise a conflict of interests between the local and foreign firms entering into the venture. The definition stated earlier emphasises the commitment of resources by both partners with their mutual interest in view. But as the enterprise progresses, areas of mutual benefit may be hard to define and the interests of the two partners may begin to diverge. Secondly, the ability of local firms to conclude joint ventures may depend on the extent and importance of the resources they have to offer. Unless the foreign firm is convinced that it has something of significance to gain by surrendering part control and ownership, it may not be interested in such ventures. Thirdly, the incentives for the foreign firm to engage in transfer-pricing practices, as a method of keeping down the share of profits accruing to the local partner, tends to be high in the case of such ventures. Also there is evidence to suggest that joint ventures pay larger royalties and technical fees for knowledge and management than wholly-owned subsidiaries.[5]

62

NATURE OF KNOWLEDGE TRANSFERRED

Available empirical evidence, mainly relating to the experience of Indian firms in the area of technical collaboration, shows that the type of knowledge transferred under licensing agreements was restricted to blueprints, designs, process sheets, flow charts and other unpatented knowledge. Transfers of human and managerial skills, or more generally corporate skills and capabilities, were rare in the case of such agreements. Transfers of such knowledge were found to be closely linked to the extent of the financial involvement of the foreign firms in the operations of the Indian firms. Although such transfers had occurred in the case of joint ventures, they were much less relative to foreign private-investment ventures.[6]

The low incidence of transfers relating to corporate skills and capabilities in the case of licensing agreements and joint ventures relative to foreign private investment is partly to be attributed to the appropriability problem discussed earlier; and partly to the nature of the transfer mechanism itself. Most modern technologies form an integral part of the corporate entity that owns them. The transferor firms may not be able to disentangle the knowledge to be transmitted from the rest of their operations. To the extent that engineering technology and managerial skills are inextricably interwoven, the effective transfer of technologies may depend on the ability of the foreign firms to operate as an integrated corporate entity. Technical-collaboration agreements deny foreign firms the kind of total participation that results from capital ownership and control over operations. As such, they may be a less effective mechanism for transferring complex modern technologies than foreign private investment.

ABSORPTIVE CAPACITY

An important determinant of the sucess of a technology transplant is the absorptive capacity of the recipient firms. This includes both their ability to implement technologies which need no alteration and their ability to restructure and adapt imported technologies to suit local conditions. The former requires managerial and labour skills at the plant level and the latter is a long-run problem involving investment in research and development. Foreign firms could be of assistance in solving both these problems. The extent of such assistance they render, however, may depend on the mode of transfer adopted. The experience of Indian firms shows that foreign firms have done little to adapt and restructure technologies transferred under the technical-collaboration agreements. It is only when they had a financial stake in the ventures abroad that they provided training and assistance in restructuring technologies.

It is likely that in the absence of assistance from the foreign firms imported know-how contributes to capital-intensity of operations and a low level of productive efficiency. Although the available empirical evidence does not permit generalisations on this issue, the evidence relating to Indian firms with technical-collaboration agreements suggests this possibility. In the electrical machinery and chemicals sector, Indian firms which had entered into technical-collaboration agreements were found to be much more capital-intensive in their operations (measured by the ratio of book value of assets to the total wage bill) than comparable foreign firms. The overall productive efficiency of foreign firms (measured by a six-year average index of total factor productivity) was also found to be higher than that of Indian firms with technical-collaboration agreements. In a three-way comparison between Indian firms with no foreign technical connections, Indian firms with technical connections and foreign firms operating in the metal products industry, Indian firms with technical connections were found to be much more capital-intensive in their operations relative to the other two groups.[7]

It is to be noted that the measurement and comparison of the relative factor intensity of different groups of firms involves several conceptual problems. The use of the ratio of assets to the wage bill as an index of factor intensity may be open to question. It could be argued that the relatively low capital intensity of the foreign firms reported in the study, cited above, may be due to the fact that they pay relatively high wage rates. This may be so. The presumption, however, is that the differences in wage rates reflects differences in labour efficiency. In other words, the wage bill would measure labour in efficiency units. The index of factor intensity referred to above, therefore, measures the ratio of capital to labour employed in efficiency units.

It could also be argued that the relatively high capital intensity of the Indian firms with foreign technical connections is due to the fact that they have ease of access to capital markets. Again this may be so. And technical-collaboration agreements with foreign firms may have strengthened their ability to raise capital on the domestic capital markets. Analogously, it can be argued that the relatively low capital intensity of the Indian firms with no foreign technical connections arises because of their relative inability to raise capital on the domestic capital markets.

These and several other reasons may have contributed to the relative capital intensity of Indian firms which had imported know-how under technical-collaboration agreements. But the point is that the technical-collaboration agreements, in one way or the other, may have contributed to the relatively high capital intensity of Indian firms which had entered into such agreements. The main factor contributing to their capital intensity, however, may be their lack of labour and managerial skills in operating imported technologies. In the absence of such skills they may have not only been inefficient in their use of capital, but may also have substituted capital for labour in the production process.

The oft-cited case of Japan's successful use of licensing agreements in her technological development also points to the importance of absorptive capacity. It is her endowments of labour skills, producer capabilities, sources of supply of materials and the assistance of the state in innovating and restructuring imported technologies that largely explains her success with licensing agreements.

The suitability of particular types of transmission mechanisms depends on the stage of development of technology-recipient economies. In the absence of supplier capabilities and human skills to restructure imported technologies, it may be in the interests of developing countries to allow for foreign financial participation. In the absence of financial investment, with its concomitant direct association and involvement, the foreign firms may have little inducement to produce the kind of technologies needed by the developing countries. As the executive of a British firm which had entered into a licensing agreement with an Indian firm put it: 'To get anything like results, a massive injection of know-how was needed; this would never be provided under a licensing agreement'.[8] The firm had entered into a licensing agreement only in the hope that it would pave the way for a joint venture.

COMPARISON OF DIFFERENT MECHANISMS OF
TECHNOLOGY TRANSFERS

This brief review of various alternative technology-transmission mechanisms for foreign private investment suggests that unpackaged transfers may neither be efficient nor feasible. It may not be efficient because of the problem of absorptive capacity. It may not be feasible because of the reluctance of foreign firms to commit the resources on the scale necessary and their inability to transfer modern technologies in an unpackaged form.

There is also no presumption that these alternative mechanisms enable developing countries to obtain the technology they need much more cheaply than under foreign private investment. In the absence of ownership of capital and control over operations foreign firms have resorted to other devices to safeguard their monopoly over technology. These relate mainly to restrictions on the use of technology imposed by foreign firms on the technology-importing firms. The most pervasive of such restrictions are those relating to restrictions on exports and sources of supply of equipment and materials. An UNCTAD study shows that out of 2,640 contracts for technology imports into twelve developing countries it examined, 47 per cent of the contracts contained export restriction clauses.[9] The recipients of technology were either prohibited from exporting the products embodying imported know-how to specified territories or they were required to obtain the prior approval of the foreign firms. In addition, foreign firms have also required the technology-recipient firms to revert to them, free of charge, the results of any research and development on imported technologies.

These restriction clauses are a device to overcome the appropriability problem discussed earlier. They provide the foreign firms with a safeguard against competition from the technology-recipient firms in third markets. Restriction clauses relating to sources of supply provide the foreign firms with an opportunity to charge a mark-up on the equipment they supply to the technology-recipient firms. Export restriction clauses are also found in joint ventures and foreign private investment ventures. In the latter case they have been imposed by the parent firms on their subsidiaries. In fact, the incidence of export-restriction clauses was found to be higher in the case of ventures involving foreign financial participiaton in India than in the case of technical-collaboration agreements.[10] But this may be an indication that the extent and nature of knowledge supplied under these agreements was relatively high.

There may be a case for arguing that such restriction

clauses should be eliminated. In the absence, however, of other methods by which the foreign firms can be assured of the returns to their investment in the production of knowledge, elimination of restriction clauses may result in heavy long-term costs in terms of a reduced flow of knowledge. On balance, the pragmatic approach for the developing countries would be to allow for foreign financial participation, but institute effective fiscal measures to garner to themselves the maximum possible benefits arising from foreign private investment.

NOTES AND REFERENCES

1.For definition and distinction between these arrangements, see Balasubramanyam, *International Transfer of Technology to India* (New York: Praeger, 1973) Ch. 2.

2.Yair Aharoni, *The Foreign Investment Decision Process* (Cambridge, Massachusetts: Harvard Business School, 1966).

3.Vaitsos, *Transfer of Resources and Preservation of Monopoly Rents, op. cit.,* p. 28.

4.J. W. C. Tomlinson, *The Joint Venture Process in International Business: India and Pakistan* (Cambridge, Massachusetts: MIT Press, 1970) p. 99.

5.John Stopford and Wells, *Managing the Multinational Enterprise* (New York: Basic Books, 1972) pp. 160-2.

6.For details see Balasubramanyam, *op. cit.,* Ch. 4.

7.*Ibid.,* Ch. 6.

8.Howard Davies, *Transnational Collaboration: a Case Study of Indo-British Technical Collaboration in the Private Sector,* unpublished M.Sc. thesis, University of Lancaster, 1974.

9.*Major Issues Arising from the Transfer of Technology to Developing Countries* (Geneva: UNCTAD Secretariat, 1974).

10.Balasubramanyam, *op. cit.,* pp. 40-1.

CHAPTER SIX

Conclusions

THE ISSUES relating to foreign private investment and technology transfer analysed in this essay pose a wide spectrum of problems for policy. These range from measures needed to increase the share of developing countries in the benefits arising from foreign private investment to the policies required to augment their technology-absorptive capacity.

BENEFIT SHARING

Monopolistic exploitation of the developing countries by the foreign firms is a recurrent theme in the literature. Exploitation is an emotionally charged expression. Strictly interpreted, exploitation arises when the profits accruing to the foreign firms are far in excess of what their costs of production and contribution to the economy justify.

This study has argued that, while there is undoubtedly an element of 'monopoly' in the profits made by foreign firms, the thesis that the high profits they make *ipso facto* amount to exploitation is exaggerated. Much of the profits the foreign firms make represent a return on their past investments in the production of knowledge. The high-profits thesis is based on a misconception of the nature of the market for knowledge and a misinterpretation of the theoretical point that knowledge is a free good (Chapters 2 and 4).

Although the organisational structure of the foreign firms contributes to the element of 'monopoly' in their profits, much of it also arises from the economic policies of developing countries. The import-substituting industrialisation policies of most developing countries have provided foreign firms with profitable domestic markets. One of the advantages claimed in favour of protectionist policies is that they attract foreign private investment. Even if this is so, it is not at all evident that foreign private investment in import-substituting industries has been socially beneficial to developing countries. Much has been written on this issue and there is no need to reiterate here the social costs of such investment, except to state that protectionist policies may have contributed to the element of monopoly in the profits made by foreign firms.

This criticism, however, applies to indiscriminate protectionist policies and not to the use of tariffs and quotas in general. Judiciously used, they can be an effective tool for regulating the activities of foreign firms. Their appropriateness in the context of the transfer-pricing problem has been discussed earlier (Chapter 3). They could also be used as a method of bargaining for a high share in the benefits arising from the operations of foreign firms. But in so doing, their other economic repercussions need to be taken into consideration.[1]

Outward-looking economic policies, which emphasise exports and resource allocation based on the comparative advantage of developing countries, may result in greater benefits from foreign private investment, although they may, at the same time, reduce the inflows of capital. In general, policies directed at increasing the degree of competition in the markets in which foreign firms operate are likely to contribute to reducing the element of monopoly in the profits of foreign firms.

TAX POLICIES

In addition to providing high levels of tariff protection,

developing countries have also attempted to attract foreign private capital by offering various tax concessions to foreign firms in the form of generous depreciation allowances and tax holidays. While the impact of such concessions on the inflow of foreign capital is not at all clear, they have served to redistribute income in favour of the foreign firms. It would be in the interests of developing countries to cooperate on fiscal policy.

Several policy recommendations, including the internationalisation of fiscal policy, discussed earlier in the paper in the context of the transfer-pricing problem, have often been made. Such a scheme, though attractive at first sight, may pose insuperable political and administrative problems. There is a need, however, for some form of cooperation among the developing countries to avoid unhealthy competition for foreign capital which may only result in the loss of tax revenues. At the very least, developing countries could agree on a common code of taxation designed to check the loss of tax revenues arising from indiscriminate tax policies. International expertise in developing and implementing efficient tax structures should also be of immense value in transferring income from foreign firms to the developing countries.

OTHER HOST-GOVERNMENT POLICIES

Most developing countries have attempted to regulate foreign private investment by imposing various restrictions on the operations of foreign firms. Many countries, including India, require that the ownership of capital by foreign firms in the subsidiaries they set up should not exceed 50 per cent. Their sphere of activity is restricted to specified industries and they are excluded from others on grounds of national interest. They are required to employ local nationals in managerial positions and there are stipulations on wage and salary structures and labour welfare.

71

While such restrictions may serve other goals, such as a reduced degree of foreign control over operations, they may also result in a lowering of the benefits arising from foreign private investment. It has been argued earlier that restrictions on majority ownership of capital impose severe limitations on technology transfer. Moreover, in the absence of majority ownership of capital and control over operation, the incentives for foreign firms to engage in transfer-pricing practices tends to be high (Chapter 5). This also applies to restrictions imposed on royalty rates and dividend repatriation. Restrictions on the activity of foreign firms, though necessary in some cases, may not always be in the interests of developing countries, especially if such restrictions provide monopoly privileges for relatively inefficient local firms. There may also be costs attached to stipulations regarding labour use and labour welfare. Indeed, foreign firms may be only too willing to comply with such regulations in return for tax concessions. As Paul Streeten, now an Economic Adviser at the World Bank, puts it: 'It is not sensible to transfer income by attempting to transform the Multinational Producing Enterprise (MPE) from what it is—a profit-seeking animal—into something it is not—a public service'.[2]

Developing countries, if they are to obtain the maximum benefit from foreign private investment, should allow majority ownership of capital by foreign firms and adopt effective tax policies to transfer income from the foreign firms. While restrictions and regulations may serve other goals they may deprive the developing countries not only of their share of income arising out of the operations of foreign firms, but also of technology.

TECHNOLOGY

Transfer of technology is the predominant theme around which discussion of most issues concerning foreign private investment revolve. One of the main criticisms of foreign firms is that they use capital-intensive technologies which are inappropriate to the labour-rich and capital-poor developing countries. This study has argued that, though this is plausible, not all of the reasons for their capital intensity can be ascribed to their 'foreignness'. Given the right incentives and opportunities to do so, foreign firms have adopted labour-intensive technologies. The incentives provided by developing countries in the form of distorted factor prices and protected product markets may be no less to blame for the adoption of capital-intensive technologies by foreign firms (Chapter 3). The basic policy recommendation in this, as in all other policy fields, is to promote competition in product markets and ensure that factor prices reflect the true social opportunity costs of factors of production.

The inappropriate-product thesis, which traces the problems of unemployment and inequalities in income distribution to the nature of products produced by foreign firms, appears to have been overdrawn (Chapter 2). The ideal solution to the problem of luxury goods produced by foreign firms is to correct the pattern of income distribution which gives rise to a demand for such goods. If this is not a feasible short-term solution, the judicious policy would be to impose high excise taxes on such goods which would deter their production.

The thesis that the nature of products produced by foreign firms gives rise to inequalities in income distribution and unemployment rests on the strong assumption that there is a unique positive relationship between products and technologies. In the light of available empirical evidence there is no strong presumption that such a relationship exists.

PROMOTION OF LABOUR-INTENSIVE
TECHNOLOGIES

While it is beyond dispute that the production and adoption of labour-intensive technologies should be encouraged, it would be injudicious to promote such

73

technologies as an end in itself. Some advocates of labour-intensive technologies appear to take the view that they are appropriate as long as they have an acceptable immediate impact on income distribution. This is a myopic view of the problem which ignores considerations of efficiency and growth. The need is for rising incomes and rising employment and not employment at any cost.

Most advocates of labour-intensive technologies have also ignored the considerable resources required to promote their production and adoption. Not least among these are the managerial and labour skills required to organise such technologies. In this sphere, foreign firms could be of assistance. Although developing countries have been active in the search for labour-intensive technologies, the multinationals, with the resources and managerial skills they possess, may be a source of immense assistance in the production of appropriate labour-intensive technologies. It is thus that this study emphasises the need for foreign-capital ownership in the ventures they undertake. In the absence of such capital ownership and control over operations, foreign firms may have little incentive to invest in the production of appropriate technologies (Chapter 5).

I have argued that unbundling the technology package may be neither feasible nor efficient (Chapter 5). The major obstacle to this, in my view, arises from the lack of technology-absorptive capacity on the part of developing countries. If other national goals, however, are an overriding consideration, licensing agreements may be an alternative to foreign private investment. The need to accelerate development being paramount, the second best alternative to foreign private investment, such as technology-transmission mechanisms, may have to be considered. But the success of such mechanisms depends on the ability of developing countries to augment their absorptive capacity. This would require a major redirection of science policy towards adaptive rather than

74

basic research. Moreover, it would also require state assistance in providing information to local firms on the alternative technologies available, their sources of supply and payments to be made for them. In this sphere, international agencies dealing with development problems could be of assistance in the collection and dissemination of information.

Lack of information appears to be a pervasive problem in foreign private investment and the transfer of technology. Many of the problems identified here such as the transfer-pricing problem, the problem of benefit sharing between foreign firms and developing countries and importation of inappropriate technologies by local firms and the adoption of capital-intensive technologies by the foreign firms, appears to arise from lack of information.[3] There is also a need to provide the multinationals with information about market conditions in the host countries. Lack of information about local factor markets, legal systems, customs and conventions can impair the efficiency of their operations.

The multinationals, for their part, may have to allow their subsidiaries to exercise more autonomy over operations than they are usually allowed to. Although the objective of systems optimisation, a key feature of the multinational enterprise, requires centralisation of operations, it may have been carried too far. Subsidiaries operating in developing countries often find themselves ham-strung by the directives issued by the parent firm. As the manager of a subsidiary colourfully puts it: 'If one is told "we do the planning, you do the doing", one's share of Napoleonic joy is ended. This comes about because of instant communications and instant travel. This dismal fate is imposed partially on the men abroad by the telephone, telex and the charms of first-class travel, tax deductible, and enhanced by the companionship of the world's choicest and most charming stewardesses . . . But the fact remains that the man in the bush knows more about it than someone shouting at him from a hovering helicopter.'[4] The man in the bush needs to be given more autonomy in taking decisions, not on overall policy, but on day-to-day operations of the firm.

CODE OF CONDUCT

The declaration on the NIEO calls for an international code of conduct for foreign firms. The UNCTAD has been active in promoting the idea. The formulation of a legally enforceable code of conduct is fraught with problems. As yet it is not clear what form such a code should take and who is to enforce it. In the absence of an understanding of what is to be regulated, formulating codes of conduct may be futile. Enunciation of vague general principles may turn out to be no more than a cosmetic operation. On the other hand, excessive and ill-designed interference with the operations of the multi-national enterprise may only serve to reduce the efficiency of its operations. The need is for policies that ensure the efficiency of its operations. As John H. Dunning, in *The Multinational Enterprise*, puts it: 'If the aim of the host country is to ensure the maximum contribution to productivity from non-resident firms, then what is most required of governments is the creation of an economic and political environment in which such firms can come nearest to achieving this by pursuing their own ends'.[5]

NOTES AND REFERENCES

1. See Corden, *op. cit.*, for a theoretical exposition of these issues.

2. Streeten, 'Costs and Benefits of Multinational Enterprises in Less Developed Countries', in Dunning (ed.), *The Multinational Enterprise, op. cit.*

3. C. Cooper, R. Dell and W. Satyaratwit, 'Choices of Techniques for Can Making in Kenya, Tanzania and Thailand', in Bhalla (ed.), *op. cit.* They report cases where foreign firms have adopted capital-intensive techniques in the absence of information on available labour-intensive techniques.

4. Thomas Aitken, *The Multinational Man* (London: Allen & Unwin, 1975).

5. Dunning, 'The Multinational Enterprise: the Background', in Dunning (ed.), *op. cit.*, p. 41.

List of Thames Essays

OCCASIONAL papers of the Trade Policy Research Centre are published under the omnibus heading of Thames Essays. Set out below are the particulars of those published to date. The first twenty-two titles were published in an octavo-size format.

1 GERARD and VICTORIA CURZON, *Hidden Barriers to International Trade* (1970), 70 pp., £1.50.

2 T. E. JOSLING, *Agriculture and Britain's Trade Policy Dilemma* (1970), 43 pp., £1.00.

3 GERARD and VICTORIA CURZON, *Global Assault on Non-tariff Trade Barriers* (1972), 40 pp., £1.50.

4 BRIAN HINDLEY, *Britain's Position on Non-tariff Protection* (1972), 64 pp., £1.50.

5 GEOFFREY DENTON and SEAMUS O'CLEIREACAIN, *Subsidy Issues in International Commerce* (1972), 64 pp., £1.50.

6 GEORGE F. RAY, *Western Europe and the Energy Crisis* (1975), 65 pp., £2.00.

7 THEODORE GEIGER, JOHN VOLPE and ERNEST H. PREEG, *North American Integration and Economic Blocs* (1975), 62 pp., £2.00.

8 HUGH CORBET, W. M. CORDEN, BRIAN HINDLEY, ROY BATCHELOR and PATRICK MINFORD, *On How to Cope with Britain's Trade Position* (1977), 80 pp., £2.00.

9   PETER LLOYD, *Anti-dumping Actions and the GATT System* (1977), 58 pp., £2.00.

10 T. E. JOSLING, *Agriculture in the Tokyo Round Negotiations* (1977), 48 pp., £2.00.

11 HARALD B. MALMGREN, *International Order for Public Subsidies* (1977), 74 pp., £2.00.

12 DAVID ROBERTSON, *Fail Safe Systems for Trade Liberalisation* (1977), 68 pp., £2.00.

13 SIDNEY GOLT, *Developing Countries in the GATT System* (1978), 40 pp., £2.90.

14 THEODOR HEIDHUES, T. E. JOSLING, CHRISTOPHER RITSON and STEFAN TANGERMANN, *Common Prices and Europe's Farm Policy* (1978), 84 pp., £2.00.

15 HANS BÖHME, *Restraints on Competition in World Shipping* (1978), 80 pp., £3.00.

16 ROBERT E. HUDEC, *Adjudication of International Trade Disputes* (1978), 92 pp., £3.00.

17 STUART HARRIS, MARK SALMON and BEN SMITH, *Analysis of Commodity Markets for Policy Purposes* (1978), 82 pp., £3.00.

18 ROBERT Z. ALIBER, *Stabilising World Monetary Arrangements* (1979), 50 pp., £3.00.

19 ROBERT L. CARTER and GERARD M. DICKINSON, *Barriers to Trade in Insurance* (1979), 72 pp., £3.00.

20 GEOFFREY SMITH, *Westminster Reform: Learning from Congress* (1979), 54 pp., £2.00.

21 W. M. CORDEN, *The NIEO Proposals: a Cool Look* (1979), 58 pp., £3.00.

22 ROBERT E. BALDWIN, *Beyond the Tokyo Round Negotiations* (1979), 64 pp., £3.00.

23 DONALD B. KEESING and MARTIN WOLF, *Textile Quotas against Developing Countries* (1980), 226 pp., £6.00.

24 M. FG. SCOTT, W. M. CORDEN and I. M. D. LITTLE, *The Case against General Import Restrictions* (1980), 106 pp., £5.00.

25 VICTORIA CURZON PRICE, *Unemployment and Other Non-work Issues* (1980), 60 pp., £3.00.

26 V. N. BALASUBRAMANYAM, *Multinational Enterprises and the Third World* (1980), 89 pp., £3.00.